C000221526

Energized Hyp

Energized Hypnosis
A Non-Book for Self Change

by
Christopher S. Hyatt, Ph.D.
&
Calvin Iwema

THE *Original* FALCON PRESS
TEMPE, ARIZONA, U.S.A.

International Standard Book Number: 978-935150-31-2
Library of Congress Catalog Card Number: 2004118432

First Edition 2005
Second Printing 2005
First Revised Edition 2007
First Original Falcon Edition 2008

Cover by Linda Joyce Franks

The paper used in this publication meets the minimum requirements of the American National Standard for Permanence of Paper for Printed Library Materials Z39.48-1984.

Address all inquiries to:
THE ORIGINAL FALCON PRESS
1753 East Broadway Road #101-277
Tempe, AZ 85282 U.S.A.
(or)
PO Box 3540
Silver Springs NV 89429 U.S.A.
website: http://www.originalfalcon.com
email: info@originalfalcon.com

Table of Contents

Introduction

When I was in grade school (c. 1954), the teacher gave the class an assignment, one you, too, may remember: we were to write down a list of "words that rhyme with." That day, the word we were to rhyme with was "bell." So, as a diligent student, I wrote down all the words I knew that rhymed with "bell": cell, dell, fell, gel, hell...and that's where I got into trouble. Suddenly, the teacher was *very* upset with me: I had written a naughty word! And even worse: I was too naive to know it was a naughty word! But I did know that she was not happy with me—and that was enough to put me into an hypnotic state. I wanted to get out of trouble so I "went inside" to find a way. And I did. I hypnotised *her* by saying there was a place called Hell's Gate near Manhattan, you could find it on any map, blah, blah, blah, and she let me off the hook.

In case you think this a quaint and dated story, flash forward fifty years to December 2004. It's the morning report on the FOX "news" network[1]. The anchorwoman is ranting and rambling about the "inappropriate language" she'd heard a reporter use on another network, but she can't bring herself to utter the offending word. Even her co-anchor can't make sense of what she's trying to say—so he asks her. You can see her making pictures in her mind, but she still can't utter the word. So she points up toward the ceiling and says, "The...opposite...of...heaven."

---

[1] Which has a well-deserved reputation for wholehearted and blatant support of "evangelical" Christianity...

After all these years, has anything changed? That anxiety-ridden, magical-thinking teacher is still terrified of "hell"—and, apparently, she expects the rest of us to pay the price for her insanity.

Mother. Sunrise. Love.
Fuck. Shit. Cunt.

Has it ever struck you how downright weird it is that the mere fact of reading or hearing (or writing!) these words evokes such a multitude of thoughts and feelings and memories? That we seem literally trapped by language and in a state of hypnosis most of the time?

But language can also be used to spring the trap. That is Hyatt and Iwema's goal with *Energized Hypnosis*: to teach you to use hypnosis to free yourself from your hypnotic state. How does he do this? In part, through information and technique. But, more importantly, by embedding the *method in the message.*

And that is what makes this a "non-book." "Books" generally purport to provide the reader with conscious *information*. But this non-book is designed to act on a much more powerful part of you: your unconscious. As you "read," you may notice that the authors deliberately move you in and out of a hypnotic state...

Word play. Deliberate mis-spellings. Odd sentence constructions.

Watch what they do to you. Let it happen. Learn...

Energized Hypnosis is the fourth pillar of Dr. Hyatt's formula for Undoing:

1) **Pillar I: Energized Meditation.** Foremost among Dr. Hyatt's books on this topic is, of course, *Undoing Yourself With* **Energized Meditation** *and Other Devices.* (As you read *Undoing Yourself,* don't forget to remember to take note of some of these valuable "other devices.") The *Techniques for Undoing Yourself* CDs and the *Radical Undoing* series of CDs and DVDs expand on (and *demonstrate!*) many of the methods described in *Undoing.* Also of great value is

To Lie Is Human: Not Getting Caught Is Divine (Dr. Hyatt's favorite). You will find other valuable techniques in *Rebels & Devils: The Psychology of Liberation*; *The Psychopath's Bible*; *The Black Book*; and *The Psychopath's Notebook.*

2) **Pillar II: Tantra** (aka Sex Magick). See *Secrets of Western Tantra: The Sexuality of the Middle Path*; *Sex Magic, Tantra & Tarot: The Way of the Secret Lover*; *Taboo: Sex, Religion & Magic*; *Tantra Without Tears*; and *Enochian World of Aleister Crowley: Enochian Sex Magick.*

3) **Pillar III: Endless Meditation** (Mahasatipatthana: the Ultimate Observer). Mahasatipatthana has been described as "the type of mindfulness that penetrates repeatedly into the body, feelings and mind, and sees the actual reality that is occurring. This is in contrast to the normal unmindful state in which the mind skips or bounces over these phenomena." Dr. Hyatt has not written much about The Endless Meditation because, as he puts it, "there just isn't much to say." You will, however, find useful information in the "You Meditation" that Dr. Hyatt presents on the *Energized Hypnosis* and *Radical Undoing* DVDs.

4) **Pillar IV: Energized Hypnosis.** In addition to this present non-book, you will find valuable techniques in *Undoing Yourself With Energized Meditation and Other Devices* (did you remember not to forget those "other devices"?), the *Techniques for Undoing Yourself* CDs, the *Radical Undoing* series of CDs and DVDs and, especially the *Energized Hypnosis* CDs and DVDs which supplement and complement this non-book. Dr. Hyatt also recommends that you read *Monsters & Magical Sticks: There's No Such Thing As Hypnosis* by Steven Heller, Ph.D. It will give you a great deal of information about how hypnosis works as well as many useful techniques. For a more academic approach, see *The Psycho-biology of Mind-Body*

Healing by Ernest Rossi, Ph.D., one of the foremost researchers in Ericksonian hypnosis.[2]

And remember: enjoy your *self* as you don't read this non-book.

— Nick Tharcher sailing somewhere
in the Caribbean, March 2007

---

[2] Hyatt worked with Rossi for four years in Los Angeles and took courses in hypnosis at the University of California at Irvine. He also is a graduate of the Hypnosis Motivation Institute.

Foreword

Regular books are designed to impart opinion, and if you are lucky, some useful information.

This is a non-book, and was deliberately designed to have an impact on you, the reader, and *to begin to create change in your life.*

You may also find that the information contained within is useful as well. As you read this non-book you will be going deeper and becoming more awake at the same time—the trick is, this non-book *is* the method, the technique......

Being a non-book about energized hypnosis, it contains language patterns similar to those used in hypnosis, so *please enjoy breaking the rules* of grammar and spelling as you read—we did.

It is imperative that you pretend you believe this is a non-book. I know it is hard to believe that since it has paper, type, a cover, etc....... As you find your brain trying to make this non-book into a book, you will discover many interesting and funny things—so please enjoy the workings of your mind, and be sure to take full advantage of your creative responses.

Every phrase in this non-book, the CDs and the DVDs has been designed for one purpose: to assist you in becoming the person you already know at some level you are. "Become who you are, there are no guarantees" is the motto.

> We strongly suggest that you get yourself a notebook or journal to keep track of your thoughts and your progress. It is very helpful to write down any thoughts, feelings and beliefs that may come up as you read.

You may notice that this non-book refers to companion audio CDs and video DVDs which are available from Falcon at http://www.originalfalcon.com.

These self-hypnosis tools will assist you in making changes along with this non-book and the work you put in. The benefits of the combination is exponentially greater than the individual components, so I suggest using them in the way described within. For best results *first read this non-book up to the point you are prompted to use the companion audios and videos, and write down what you are asked to write down. And follow the instructions regardless of how silly they seem to you.*

This combined program is designed to work at multiple analytic and synthetic levels...much of the work takes place —out—of—awareness.

Its purpose is to provide the perspective and methodology to change any behaviors and beliefs which are **now** *unacceptable* to **You**.

From time to time as you read and re-read this non-book you might notice your mind drifting, eyes blinking, a feeling of relaxation, a twitch or two, or even a sense of annoyance. Whatever you sense or feel, simply allow it to happen.

I know that at some point it will become obvious to you that the patterns that develop from our interaction will satisfy more than your curiosity. What makes this all work so well for *you* is the knowledge that there is something beyond what can be known verbally, that has and will continue to guide you to the solutions that are being revealed to you by *that* part of you and your in-depth awareness.

The Non-Section

Chapter 1

Going Deeper...NOW

I remember a friend telling me about a hypnosis training he had attended. The trainer was talking about his work with Milton Erickson, who is considered by many to be the grandfather of hypnosis. He had the ability to look into your eyes and communicate with a very deep part of you, almost as if he was speaking directly with your soul. "There is a part of you that has been taking care of *you*, for many years. It is the part of you that keeps your heart beating, that digests your food, that blinks your eyes, and it knows much more about you than I ever will. And *your unconscious* knows exactly, *now, that I am speaking directly to it*, and *it can respond in the most appropriate way for **you**.*" And with that comment, he closed his eyes and felt the most incredible sense of being *understood and acknowledged* at a very deep level, and as that feeling welled up and a tear formed in his eye, he realized that this experience would *make changes that ripple out into the future*. "Because I want that part of you to know, that I know, just how hard it has worked for you, and I want to thank that part of you directly, because I know that for you to change, *your unconscious is going to help you out quite a bit*."

And after that, my friend said that an hour had passed by the time he had opened his eyes again, and although he didn't remember much of what was said, he had the distinct feeling that allowed him to know, for the first time in a long time, that *things will be changing for the better*. He said to me, "The feeling is like hope, yet it goes beyond that. It is a kind of deep, inner knowing, and even if you don't understand it fully at the time, that *other-than-conscious part* of you *knows* how and *when it is being communicated with* and *can powerfully assist you. Now* I don't know about you, but that *sounds pretty good to me*, doesn't it?"

I could tell that my friend had indeed learned a lot and made some real progress at that training, and was glad to have recommended it.

There is a phrase that is heard in some hypnosis circles that says "either all communication is hypnosis, or none of it is."

> If you see what we mean, smile and nod your head yes...... If you don't feel a deep sense of what was said, take three very deep breaths and sigh.

All of our communication influences both others and ourselves. For example, at some point in your life you have felt the sun on your skin.

Recently I was lying on a beach in the tropics, underneath a palm with my toes in the sand...

The water was a brilliant blue color, sharply contrasting the white hulls of the sailboats in the distance...

As the wind gently rustles the leaves, and cools you, as you feel the heat from the sun on your skin...

The smell of the ocean is so distinct you can taste the salt on your lips...

Stop for a moment and realize that as you were reading, you were representing what I was saying internally.

> If you sense this, squeeze your left thumb with your right hand; if not take 2 deep breaths and sigh.

You might have pictured the scene in your mind or felt the warmth on your skin. You might have started talking to yourself, inside your mind.

If you re-read the previous paragraph, you will notice that all of your five senses were brought into play. Which ones did you notice the most? Which one the least? How much more relaxed are you now?

If 100 people read this paragraph, each would create a different arrangement of the cues that would help them to create, remember and re-experience these sensations.

This is the effect of communication *and* hypnosis. Some of you might acknowledge this fact by nodding your head. Others might say to yourself "that makes sense," while still others need do nothing.

> As you start to digest these familiar ideas, some of them may be appealing and be things that you want to remember. Write them down in your notebook or journal.

Each of us has style, and at one time or another each of us has changed our style to suit the needs and desires of the present. We are not talking about fashion, but about self-style.

You have your own style of communicating with yourself and others and for interacting with your environment.

You have created and chosen this style. Many of us have done this with intention while others have chosen just to let it happen. You even have your own style of problems, difficulties and limitations that you have chosen. But **NO**, you firmly reply, *I* did not choose to have these. *I* did not ask to include *those* things in my personal(ity) style. Maybe you did not choose them deliberately, or remember them now consciously, and simply realize that this time, RIGHT NOW IS *YOUR* TIME......*it is your turn* to begin to *define your self on your own terms.*

> If you agree, show it in your eyes, let them light up; if not, pull your shoulders to your ears and hold that position for a minute or so, drop them and say No, thank you.

If you would like to improve your style, to enhance your effect, and to find a spot in yourself somewhere where you could look out with curiosity and certainty; or, on the other hand, if you would simply like to learn, then you have made the correct choice in buying this non-book. It will shed some light on how you work so you can make adjustments to your style. You can take a deeeeep breath and *decide to design and redesign your self*, and *begin to choose* how you respond and interact with yourself, others and your environment, instead of simply re-acting (acting again).

If you have found yourself re-acting out the same stories and patterns of the past, and would *like* to *do and feel something better*, then become aware of what you are looking at right now. What you are holding in your hand is your gateway into your deeper self—it is a living trance.

> Get up, jump up and down three times and shout, "Yes I will......" If you don't want to, gently shake your head no, or if that doesn't please you, do nothing.

This non-book will also help you review secret and sometimes painful feelings and beliefs calmly, peacefully and privately in your mind, and then *come to new decisions about them*.

To begin this journey would you now please change your body position in some way or, if you prefer, move to a special place where you had your last pleasant experience.

Make yourself comfortable, the way you do when you watch a favorite movie or the big game, because the game you find yourself playing at this very moment—the game of life—is worth winning...if you so choose.

Chapter 2

A Little Bit About How Things Work

During our Psycho-Physical journey you will be asked to explore new ideas, new perspectives and perform certain tasks; but before we reach that point it is important for you to understand what Psycho-Physics really is.

Psycho-Physics is, first, the relationship between mind and body.

Every mental action has a physical consequence and every physical action has a mental consequence.

Research has not yet found where the mind stops and the body begins, although you may have thought of them as separate.

Second, Psycho-Physics is the relationship between person and environment, where every environment affects the person and every personal act affects the environment. Through an understanding of these interrelationships, you will begin to build the foundation upon which change (and your life) will be built.

The mind-brain develops over a period of time and contains many associations that have formed through learning.

Many of these complex associations occur primarily in childhood before the age of 7–8. Before this age, the mind-brain has not yet developed the critical-analytical capabilities of differentiation and evaluation, thus making cortical intervention into autonomic reactivity difficult if not impossible. This means that the child is not rationally deciding whether or not the association or generalization is useful or makes logical sense.

One of our significant learning achievements is the acquisition of language and the related assignment of meaning.

A common metaphor for this is that we build an **internal map** for meaning and relationship of all that we experience.

It is of prime importance to note that much of this learning takes place *before logical and rational thinking ability develops.*

The map is not the territory. A highway map of Arizona has lots of information about that area. Its purpose is to help you get from one place to another, to help you get where you want to go. It is designed to sort and present the necessary information *in line with the purpose it was created for.* After studying and using that map long enough, one becomes confident about that information, one believes it to be real and true. But it will **not** prepare you for encountering a rattlesnake, which is also quite real. You can imagine then, that it makes sense to update your map now to include new and useful information.

Your internal map of yourself is not yourself, and it probably could use a little updating.

To repeat:

Your internal map of yourself is not yourself, and it probably could use a little updating.

If you agree, close your eyes and let your mind drift wherever it wants to go. Let it go now and begin to sense your body. When it is time, return to the non-book. If you don't agree, take four big breaths and sigh with relief.

One of the important logical abilities that is lacking in the child is the concept of reversibility.

This is the understanding that, by reversing an operation, the effects are returned to their original condition (in most cases). An example: a child sees that a lettuce leaf has been placed on his sandwich and believes the sandwich is now ruined. Even when the offending lettuce has been removed, the sandwich is still mysteriously tainted, and he will not eat it. The child is not trying to be difficult—in fact, the brain has not developed enough yet to understand!

This means that without critical and analytical ability, many meanings are assigned and beliefs are formed that 1) we did not consciously choose, 2) were extremely limited due to lack of information and understanding and, 3) are often still operational in adulthood.

The *meanings and beliefs are in your map.* Your map is not reality, it is only a representation of reality. It is a tool. You created your map in such a way that it may not be the best map to get you where you want to go *right now.* If you *update your map,* you will be *better equipped for your journey.* Keep in mind that most feelings are also part of your map, and if you lift up the covers you will often find beliefs hidden underneath.

Stretch and take 5 deep breaths, close your eyes and tell yourself out loud what you see.

The drawing of a fire truck made by a five-year-old will not help a trainee fireman learn how to operate a real truck.

It is not the five-year-old's fault, it does not make him bad. It just does not contain the same amount of, or type of, information that a technical training manual does.

Realize that in many ways the way in which you view yourself and your capabilities and possibilities is exactly the same as the five-year-old's drawing. **Keep the passion... Update the information.**

You might begin to think of more important and far-reaching consequences of this stage of learning, especially around negative and limiting beliefs and feelings of inadequacy and guilt.

You might now start feeling a sense of relief, because you did the best you could at the time, and right now *you can decide for yourself when is **now** the time to re-decide.*

Children often deify their parents as they are growing up, and tend to look at adults as "the big people who know how to do things." They do not have the logical ability or perspective to understand that their parents are often inaccurate or simply ineffective humans. Because of this, beliefs and concepts such as "If they are right, I must be wrong..." or "They are good so I must be bad" develop. Young children do not understand what it "means" to lose a job, to fight with a spouse, or to get drunk. They are easily frightened, confused and overwhelmed by their emotions. If an empowering explanation isn't offered, a child will assign meaning on their own...and most often it will be about them. And worse, it will often be in error—yet most people have strict *fidelity* to their childhood conclusions. Most people will fight like hell to hold on to beliefs, conclusions, assumptions and feelings which limit them and cause them deep pain.

If you are ready to let go...take three breaths and shout yes; if you wish to hold on, you may, take three breaths and grasp your left arm.

To further add to this, parents seldom encourage their children to question them and to look for more accurate and useful information.

In fact, the child's willingness to believe their parents is exactly how most parents control them. They may not intend for their children to adopt painful and limiting beliefs about themselves, but it happens nonetheless.

Just because a bad or unpleasant set of events has occurred and a behavior originated to cope with these events before the mind was fully developed does not mean that anyone must remain victimized by either the painful experience or the adaptive behavior. This holds for both acute and chronic conditions.

For example, a young child I know was constantly and publicly compared to a relative who everyone claimed was more intelligent than he was. When he was placed into a learning situation the anxiety he experienced prevented him from recalling and verbalizing information. Therefore, since it is assumed that intelligence is reflected by the ability to memorize, recall and verbalize information, he and everyone else believed he was stupid.

> What is the useful purpose of the belief of being stupid, you ask. It could be that it was necessary to agree with being stupid to be accepted by those who were threatened by anything greater than themselves. In a young mind, and in most pack animals, acceptance often equals survival. (This is a good example of a belief or behavior serving a *useful purpose* in some past context.)

As he frequently failed he began to ignore school and dropped out at age 16. If you were to review his grades you would find that he was a D+ to C- student and that even his IQ scores were low normal. At the age of 17 he joined the Navy, and on the first exam scored the highest out of 80 men, some of whom were college graduates. When they called out his name the Chief Petty Officer stated that he couldn't believe it was him and that he must have cheated. Thereafter, he never scored over a C again.

When he left the Navy he took the High School and College GED. Not only did he pass the High School GED, but also received 18 college units which included subjects such as chemistry, physics, English, math, social science and psychology. Besides having received low scores in these subjects while in school, he never even finished the last two years of high school. He was never aware that he understood these subjects, and even though he was completely unable to verbalize the information, he performed well enough to pass the tests. Of course when his family found out that he had passed they explained it as luck or cheating.

> It is worth noting **now** that this young man went on to earn two M.A. and two Ph.D. Degrees, as well as being published many times. *What will **you** accomplish with your new resources and through the changes you are making **now**?*

This account demonstrates that learning did take place at some level and was, in fact, encoded. The fact that he couldn't recall the information was due to the type and chronic nature of anxiety that he felt when he was put on the spot. The effect of this *anxiety* (which is *another form of information and self-communication*) interfered with his ability to recall and verbalize the information. When he was placed in a different learning situation—that of taking an exam with strangers who would not know how he did— the tension lessened enough to allow him to access the information and write it down. Yet, for the life of him, he couldn't recall the same information verbally and publicly five minutes after the exam. For example, when a friend asked him about the questions on the exam immediately after completing it, he couldn't even remember *one*. He had a form of amnesia. Could it have been that the amnesia functioned solely to maintain the belief of stupidity?

> This story is a good example of how someone else suggested that test anxiety "meant" stupidity…and how easy it can be to adopt erroneous beliefs, simply because other people said so. *What **false beliefs** do you have about you, that when you **drop them**, will **create relief and freedom**?*

> Tonight, when you drop off to sleep and are dreaming, you may remember 1 or 2 beliefs you may wish to be rid of.

Chapter 3

More About How Things Work: Your Brain

Although we like to fancy ourselves as rational beings, we are inherently irrational.

The truth is simple: we are irrational beings capable of rational thought. Have you ever wondered why so many people know so much about "what to do" and why so few actually do it? This relates to being overweight or in debt, problem relationships, parenting, career success, etc.

There has never been more information available, yet the lack of application seems to be culturally universal. There are some things worth understanding about your own brain that will shed some light on this.

What and how we learn is fundamentally dependent on the neuro-biochemical state of the learner at the time of the learning experience. This is known as "state dependent learning," which is the tendency for one to realize the effects of learning more in the special conditions associated to the learning experience than in other conditions and contexts.

Have you ever noticed that you remember more of unique and emotionally charged experiences than you do of the average and uneventful ones?

One of the most obvious and clear examples of state dependent learning is traumatic amnesia. The person in his normal state cannot recall the events of the trauma, yet under hypnosis or during sleep the events and emotions are clearly experienced.

People have different resources and memories due to the emotional state they find themselves in.

Less obvious but common examples of this intriguing psycho-physical relationship are the day to day "losses" of memory. Maybe you have had the experience of forgetting something simple like the name of the movie you watched the night before. Most likely you have had the experience of walking into a room and forgetting what it was you needed, only to return to the room you just came from and remember it.

Researchers have been studying "mood modules." The concept of mood modules suggests that, for different emotional states, we have different memories and access to different internal resources.

As you learn, your brain develops biochemical neural bonds (BCNBs). These bonds are the neural connections in your brain that enable the signal to travel from neuron to neuron, creating the link from stimulus to response. Some behavioral scientists have called some of these responses "conditioned emotional reactions." The bonds are physical in nature, and could be viewed metaphorically as "wiring connections." A simplified example would be learning to walk. Your nervous system takes in information about height, speed, and balance through your senses, and then translates and transmits that information to your muscles. As you practice, those connections that enable the most efficient and stable movements are reinforced, and the behavior is "grooved in." Throwing a ball with your nondominant hand will show you the difference between a conditioned behavior and a new one.

Bonds are also created within and between the emotional and thinking centers of the brain. Many of these bonds are formed before the critical-evaluative mind was fully developed and could rationally intervene. Most fear and anxiety are learned habits created at this time.

To repeat:

Most fear and anxiety are learned habits created at this time.

Another form of learning is imprinting.

Imprint theory states that at critical times during early development, or periods of imprint vulnerability, strong bonds are created as a result of one-time-learning.

Researchers such as Konrad Lorenz have studied this in animals, and have documented cases where a baby gosling was exposed to a ping-pong ball shortly after birth and imprinted it as "mommy." It then followed the ball around, nestled with it, and later in life attempted to mate with white round objects.

Although this research has not been studied extensively with humans, the possible similarities are worth thinking about.

You can imagine a young girl, who was very excited about peeling an orange by herself for the first time.

As she was proudly demonstrating her new skill and ability, her mother was looking past her out the window and, upon seeing the neighbor's kid digging up her flower garden, screamed "NOooo"; then, in her excited state, accidentally knocked the coffee pot over, spilling hot coffee on the young child's head, which caused her to fall down the stairs and make a trip to the hospital for stitches. Now, as a 27-year-old woman, she dislikes oranges and the color orange, and feels extremely uneasy when doing new things for the first time, to the point of avoiding new activities.

The important thing to remember is that every behavior, belief or habit has at one time protected you, even though *it may now be a hindrance to your development*. Since these bonds and beliefs are *now* unacceptable to you, *they may be replaced if you choose* with new, creative and more flexible survival (or even trivial) strategies.

In addition to the lagging development of the rational and logical faculties, the protracted state of dependency and defenselessness of the human infant make it highly susceptible to imprinting and early learning. Besides important learnings happening "randomly," the errors and irrationality of the previous generation are easily passed forward and *the child comes to its own conclusions by itself which are often flawed and difficult to retrieve and restructure.*

To repeat:

The child comes to its own conclusions by itself which are often flawed and difficult to retrieve and restructure.

> The above insight alone is worth the price of this non-book. Consider that most psychologists and counselors have no sense of this idea: that the child's own erroneous or incomplete conclusions can be the cause of present day disturbances. Can you think of a conclusion you came to as a child which was either wrong or incomplete? How is it affecting you today?

The belief that the educational system can modify these early errors and innate tendencies is more a dream than a reality. (If knowledge alone were adequate, no one would have any "problems."). The so-called "socialization" process—which is innate for humans—simply disguises what is really going on and thereby makes it more difficult to *redesign and recover yourself.*

We are raised to be "similar" to our parents to fill the roles that are "appropriate" and to do things the way they have always been done. This isn't necessarily done out of malice, but rather without ever questioning its usefulness.

(Most people never *really* question what they are doing—they simply follow along and scorn those who do not, simply out of habit.) Thinking on one's own is not usually encouraged, and young minds cannot distinguish useful information from dogma. This wouldn't be so bad if it weren't increasingly difficult to erase or modify the dogma as the organism matures.

Guilt, shame, abandonment and the withholding of love and support work well at producing the necessary stimuli to keep a child "in line."

It may appear to a young mind then that certain behaviors "cause" these uncomfortable emotions. In actuality it is the adults' own beliefs and responses that are responsible. This is not evident to the child who does not have the necessary perspective, rational and logical ability to "*see through this*" yet.

You have probably heard a parent say to a child, "You think you're smart, don't you?"—as if it is a bad thing to be smart. Then, later on, when the child gets to school and doesn't do well, everyone shrugs their shoulders. The child simply learned that being smart felt bad. Now the expectations of being smart are in conflict with the need to fit in.

This example may seem over-simplified and naive, but you would be surprised at how many times these types of things come up in hypnosis. Now apply this to sex, religion, race, money, physical ability, interpersonal relationships and career choices and you will begin to see the far-reaching implications of what you have been reading about.

You might ask why it is so difficult to remove these bonds when they are no longer useful. One reason is that each bond is *physical in nature*. Each bond has a biochemical and neural basis that has been strengthened by the fact that at one time or another it has served a useful purpose and has been repeated over and over again. If the environment once continued to demand these patterns and habits for the purpose of survival, they have now been conditioned into "necessary" and "essential" behaviors and beliefs.

Another reason is that those parts of your brain that govern survival and the lower instincts have already matured. Your brain is no longer developing at the rate it once was. This is no different than why your bones stop growing at a certain age. It sometimes takes more effort to make changes than it did to initially learn.

The third reason, which we will go into in depth, is that there seems to be some basic design problems in the human brain structure. These human design elements are worth looking into because understanding them will allow you to *see yourself in a new light, so you can take yourself off the hook,* and get down to business and begin to make the changes that you wish to make.

The first design consideration is that the frontal lobes, which govern executive functioning and rational and logical thinking, are easily influenced by the lower brain. On the other hand, the frontal lobes have much less influence on the lower brain. In other words, more information is sent from the lower brain up than from the higher brain down. The consequences of this is that even though you "know better," the lower brain has more influence over your choices and behavior.

A basic example of this can be seen in optical illusion. Imagine that you have your face pressed against the clear window of a racquetball court. Even though your front brain "knows" that the ball cannot hurt your eyes, when you see the ball coming toward you, you flinch strongly nonetheless. Your lower brain, or what is sometimes called the older brain, contains the neurological circuits responsible for the safety of the organism, and these override the rational process.

STOP STOP STOP

A MODEL OF THE BRAINS.
USE IT DAILY.

> Before you read what follows, blink at least a half dozen times and draw your attention to your nose...... As the tip of your nose becomes clear, notice how your eyes tire...... If you can do this for 5 minutes you may find yourself in a mild trance, opening your mind wider and wider to what will follow.

The parts of the brain associated with emotional activity are closest to the memories of human relationships; next closest are those associated with animals; and then come the memories associated with tools. What are the implications?

Background

A current, and aging, paradigm describes the human brain as a tripartite entity:

1. The reptile brain = oldest
    a. Brain stem
    b. The most functional part of the reptile brain
    c. Concerned with basic survival
    d. Blood pressure, endocrine, thirst, breathing, heart rate regulator.
    e. Not so much emotional as parametrically reactive to ensure survival.
    f. If you step on a rattlesnake's tail and it bites you, it's probably not mad, it's just reacting.
2. The mammalian brain = evolutionarily newer
    a. Limbic region
    b. More developed in mammals than reptiles
    c. Adds the emotional tinge, halo, and connection to every event.
    d. Emotions make events more intense which can aid survival. Memory storage becomes more efficient.
    e. If you step on a tiger's tale and it bites you, you can be sure it's emotionally upset and angry.
3. The human brain = very evolutionarily new—we don't even know how to use it...yet.

a. The cortex/neocortex
b. Very newly evolved
c. Allows higher processes: planning, analysis, scheming, math, art, science, religion, meditation.
d. If you step on my tail, I may smile at you, but I am secretly planning your murder to be carried out in 6 months.

Analysis

If we consider the emotions to be older than memories, and closer to the center of the brain, we can postulate that as one moves laterally and outward from the brain stem one encounters more advanced, intelligent, aware, awake, and newly-evolved portions of the brain. However awareness, enlightenment and so-called higher functions are not at all necessary for survival or procreation. In fact, the basic survival portion of the brain is the brain stem. From there we tack on enhancements like emotions and then cognition. While cognitive processes can enhance quality of life, they are superfluous for survival. So, the basic point is that the nearer to the brain stem/reptile brain we get, the more essential for survival the brain segment becomes. For example, if we shut down the portions of your frontal cortex, "you" are gone; however, your body and a different personality will live on quite functionally.

Thus, the conclusion is: the fact that the social memory is closer to the limbic and brain stem regions may indicate that sociality and social relationships have been more important for species-survival than higher cognitive functions like the manipulation and construction of tools. Therefore, the human being as a species is prioritized as follows: first, reflexive; second, emotional/social; and third, logically intelligent. Any intelligent thoughts you have will travel from the cortex to be filtered by the emotions, then the brain stem—meaning you, the "you" that you really are in the ivory tower of your cortex, is constantly modified and altered by the emotions and the watchful eye of the brain stem. You are being monitored by the ancient parts of our species—you are being kept in line with our ancient species' goals.

<> *YOU CAN WAKE UP NOW* <>
IF YOU WISH

Key to self-change: Realize that new thinking, which takes place in the frontal lobes, takes time to reprogram the lower brain.

Martial arts are taught with this principle in mind. In defensive and combat situations thinking isn't useful, so they drill in responses until they become second nature and automatic. You want to do the same thing with the beliefs and behaviors about yourself that you really want.

The second design anomaly of the human brain is that the frontal lobe, or higher brain, is bypassed under periods of stress. If you step off the curb and notice that a speeding bus is bearing down on you, you jump out of the way without "thinking about it."

The lower brain centers not only talk to and influence the higher brain centers, but also talk within and between themselves. This means that, while early conditioning can be modified, under intense stress the lower centers activate previous learning within and between the lower brain centers.

Key to self-change: Realize that at times your old responses may surface.

This doesn't mean that you aren't changing—it's just how your brain works to protect you. Keep working at your changes and on your goals until they become second nature.

The third design anomaly is that the parts of the brain where memories are stored are at varying distances from the part of the brain that governs emotional activity. But remember: the memories closest to the emotional centers are those associated with human relationships, the next closest are memories related to animals, and the next are the memories associated with tools. Research on the brains of stroke victims show the memory centers associated with lower social brain activity are *physically* closer to the emotional brain than memories associated with tools.

One consequence of this could be that our relationships with others does have a greater impact on our emotions than our relationships with tools.

If you consider rational thought, goal setting and planning as tools, it begins to make sense why other people can "short-circuit" your best intentions. This may explain why we act so oddly and "irrationally" around certain people. Throughout history, being excommunicated from the "tribe" often resulted in death. Therefore it makes sense, from a survival standpoint, for your brain to be designed this way to enhance the odds of survival.

Key to self-change: Remember that, although others affect you, they don't determine your worth, capabilities or possibilities...*you can and will do.*

The next paragraph is one of the most important you may ever read. Set a date when you **begin to apply it everyday**. Don't forget to remember. Lift your head as high as you can and scratch your chin three times or more if it feels good. When you are done reading this paragraph, treat yourself to something you like...... Now, begin to read it SLOWLY...... Now read it faster and faster and faster and faster......take three deep breaths and let go—NOW!

The last design consideration is that the mind has a difficult time differentiating between subjective internal reality and external objective reality. Your senses take in information from the outside world and your brain responds to it. Your brain also responds to your imagination. Think about how real and scary (or sexy) your dreams can be. What often happens is that your body responds to your subjective internal thinking processes and produces emotions which are "proof" that this is taking place in your objective reality "out there."

To repeat:

The last design consideration is that the mind has a difficult time differentiating between subjective internal reality and external objective reality. Your senses take in information from the outside world and your brain responds to it. Your brain also responds to your imagination. Think about how real and scary (or sexy) your dreams can be. What often happens is that your body responds to your subjective internal thinking processes and produces emotions which are "proof" that this is taking place in your objective reality "out there."

Can out there be in here and can in here be out there? How do you know which is which and who is who?

Stamp your foot three times if you agree; if not, don't move for 3 minutes.

Many children "know" that monsters live under their bed and in their closet. They are sure that they are there; even though they can see that they are not there, they are still afraid.

When you ask them what they are picturing and hearing inside their mind (which happens as fast as a thought and is outside their conscious awareness), they will give you detailed descriptions and scenarios of the monsters and how scary they are. They have trouble differentiating between the reality inside their mind and the reality "out there," just like adults do. When you think about how real their emotions are...*remember, most adults are hallucinating monsters...*

Key to self-change: Remember that some of your emotions come from your previous learning patterns and not from objective reality. *Realize that oftentimes the only thing*

that stands between you and what you want are those emotions.
Emotions can be as real as brick walls...

It can be useful to *realize that most of our difficulties in life*
stem from the fact that our brain is designed the way it is, rather
than from some underlying deficiency in our value and
worth. (These "underlying deficiencies" live in the closet
and under the bed, by the way.)

The very nature of these design elements at one time
was a great asset, and is now (most of the time) a weakness
that needs to be overcome. The brain seems to be designed
to guarantee survival first, but there is a difference between surviving and thriving—which is what this non-
book is about. Since your brain doesn't automatically
change its structure (in the way we desire) as we learn and
grow, you need to *learn to do this yourself...deliberately.*

> If you agree that many of your emotions and feelings are
> learned and have underlying beliefs, the next time you feel
> overwhelmed by an emotion, forget to remember that you
> know what is going on. Act as if you have no control over
> what is going on in here and out there.

As you begin to understand how your mental-
emotional state affects you, you will begin to *realize how*
*important it is to **access and maintain useful emotional***
states.

> You can remember a time when you were depressed, and
> while you were *doing* that, you tended to view all of your
> past experiences as rotten and miserable and your present
> and future opportunities the same. And then, when you
> were happy, everything in the past, present and future
> seemed just right. How useful will it be for you to **remember**
> **this** the next time you are feeling other than you would like to
> be.

Even as an adult, now that the critical mind can intervene, it can be difficult to change these bonds. You might

notice the various ways that people attempt change (e.g., medicate themselves) and the preponderance of drug use in avoiding emotions. You may also have heard of the use of drugs in shamanistic and eclectic circles to change these bonds. You might wonder how can we change biochemical-neural bonds without the use of drugs.

(Psycho-pharmacological) medications are extremely popular now. You may have seen the commercials with little happy-smiley balls who no longer have a care in the world. These drugs are often helpful for stabilizing, but the problem (as with other common self-medications) is that they don't change the underlying bonds reliably.

Put your mind at ease. The fact that the cause of all difficulties are biochemical-neural bonds gives us hope since the brain is always growing, re-evaluating and re-programming itself. Since the brain is not fixed, most anything that has been created can be changed if you simply know how.

The latest brain research doesn't support the false, but common, belief that just because events once seriously damaged or affected one's life that they should and will continue to affect it. The reason why external drugs are not essential for change to take place is because the brain is a gigantic biochemical manufacturing plant. It is your own pharmacy and you are the pharmacist. You can access the pharmacy through new thoughts and new behaviors that create new learnings. Through repetition and over time they will cause you to feel different; you may, if you choose, realize that this means you are changing!

It is a widely known and accepted fact that almost all medication does not work directly on the body, but simply affects the nervous system, which in turn creates its own biochemicals that go to work on the problem.

This discussion about how biochemical-neural bonds and your brain structure cause much of your misery may make you depressed.

If it does, *STOP.*

Take a deep breath and relax. You can start to feel the relief that comes from understanding yourself better, which makes your path to self change much easier, because *you no longer have to fight yourself. Now* you can focus your energy and efforts on doing what works.

People are so often focused on the quick fix and the silver bullet that they get discouraged easily. Society sells you the hope of something-for-nothing at every turn. We all like and enjoy peak experiences, but it's really the focus and repetition that will make it happen for you. Realize that it takes time, energy and commitment to *develop yourself and change your style.* **You are worth the investment.**

The purpose of this non-book is to provide you with the opportunity and the tools to reclaim your emotional and psychological self. Although it might have *seemed* like an impossible task *in the past,* it is good to note that if some changes take a little longer than others, realize it is just part of your psycho-physical makeup. *Realize that you are dealing with your brain structure and the impact of your previous learning, not your value or your ability to change.*

If while reading you had any realizations about yourself, or if any old memories popped up, write them down in your notebook or journal.

Chapter 4

Different Is OK

Most present day fears are now useless.

At one time these fears may have had utility, but the only purpose they serve now is to give you a sense of *familiarity*.

Although the fears are painful, they give you a sense of confidence because they are familiar and have continuity with the past. The difficulty in changing many of them is that a primitive sense of identity has been created around them. You will notice I said "sense of identity" and not "identity." Real identity is innate, and exists without clinging to old beliefs and the behaviors that support them.

> Many financial traders have stated that they finally started making money and became successful when they were able to *give up the need to be "right"* and started measuring results based on *what* **works,** instead of believing what other people told them was good and bad or right and wrong.

You are not your feelings.

You are not your thoughts.

You are not your job, your relationship, your current situation.

You are not your problems and limitations. Right now, in the present moment, in the *hear* and *now,* sitting there, reading this non-book, *you are pure potential.*

Proof experiment: Look around, become aware that there is a you, sitting in a room, reading. The moment before I made you aware of this, you may have been lost in reading. There was no distinction between you and the process of reading, there was only reading. Now, pinch your leg. Notice that you can observe your *feeling* pain. You, the observer, *are not* the *pain*. How can you be, if *you* are observing it.

Are you there?

If you want to try this, let yourself become overwhelmed any time you like...... Then hold your breath and see how long your identity depends on your beliefs, feelings, ideas, relationships or, for that matter, anything else.

Of course, you don't have to wait, *you can do it right now*...... Build up a thought image that is very important to you, *now* hold your breath and *begin to see what happens*. Remember, hold it as long as you can and then...hold it again—**now** *let go*. Shake your head yes if you agree; sigh with relief if you don't.

Once you know that you can replace your restrictive and painful survival strategies with useful, creative and expansive strategies, you will stop clinging to the familiar old patterns and let go of them. In fact, often the only benefit of the limiting old patterns is the comfort in familiarity. *Fidelity* to the familiar is only a way to cope, and there is a big difference between coping and excelling.

You might picture yourself having been thrown into the deep end.

The familiar, limiting way of dealing with this is to thrash about, barely keeping your head above water. Another way is to trust and learn to swim, thereby gaining freedom and the ability to enjoy the pool of life and swim wherever you want to go.

As you replace and remove what you have decided is no longer useful, you will begin to elicit personal power in yourself that will extend to others. As your personal power expands and grows, your capabilities and options will multiply on their own accord, and your momentum will enable you to accomplish your goals and reach your dreams. This is the process behind the saying "The rich get richer and the poor get poorer."

---

*You **can**, can't you?* The word *can* implies ability or permission. Right now *you* are learning how to *have the ability*.
    Give yourself permission, RIGHT NOW. You are all grown up, so you don't need anyone else to tell you what you can and can't do with your own mind anymore. Being a child—still—is a habit—which you CAN ***give up*** NOW—little by little—or in one or two steps.

Will You Reject Your Newfound Freedom?

Consider this analogy.

A person has a bad kidney.

If he doesn't get it replaced he will die or live a severely restricted life. His first step is to ***decide to*** go in for surgery and then a new kidney is implanted. The body starts to reject the healthy kidney. Why? Because it is *different* and foreign to the body. Even though the kidney is needed for the body's survival, it begins to destroy the new kidney. To intervene and stop the body from destroying the new kidney, the physician gives the patient drugs that prevent the body from rejecting it. One way the drugs work is to *"fool"* the body into believing that the kidney is not alien. Another way is to reduce the rejection response itself. The doctor also prescribes a regiment of healing activities.

It is up to the patient to ***engage in the new activities*** in order to get better. In time the body heals and accepts the new kidney as it own. The person then goes on to live a healthier life.

Many people are trained to feel bad when they are faced with doing something different. (This, as you have guessed by now, is what *fidelity to the past* means.) The patient may have felt bad that the original kidney didn't work out, but he soon was able to *realize that feeling bad didn't help*. It is of extreme importance, to *become aware of this* and *change your beliefs about "different"* so that you can *feel good about changing.*

Just suppose for a minute that all of the things you want in your life are different than what you are currently thinking, feeling and doing. Now you see, hear and feel the importance of why it is necessary for you to *be comfortable and powerful in the face of new and different people, situations and learnings.*

Much of the rapport between humans is based on similarity. We are trained to believe that sameness—being similar—is good and that being different is bad. We are trained to accept the beliefs and standards of our parents and peer groups. Most mammals are trained to be highly sensitive to difference. Robert Anton Wilson quotes Robert Ardrey in his book *Prometheus Rising...*

"Imagine that you are a monkey and you're running along a path...and unexpectedly meet face to face another animal. Now, before you know whether to attack it, to flee it, or to ignore it, you must make a series of decisions. Is it monkey or non-monkey? If non-monkey, is it pro-monkey or anti-monkey? If monkey, is it male or female? If female, is she interested? If male, is it adult or juvenile? If adult, is it of my group or some other?...You have about one fifth of a second to make all these decisions, or you could be attacked."

I'm sure you can think of examples of this in your own life. How many instances do you know of where someone decides to be *different* and gets a better education than their parents; or changes religions; or marries outside of their ethnic group causing an emotional rift like a tidal wave in their family? WHO ARE YOU REJECTING BY BECOMING MORE SUCCESSFUL? The list may be longer than you think.

> An infamous financial trader once said that the reason most people fail as traders is the human tendency to do what feels comfortable and familiar instead of doing what works.

It seems that people have the tendency to sort by familiarity and consistency. To their own detriment they often choose to surround themselves with people, places and activities that they are familiar with and which remain relatively stable and constant—even though they do not provide them with the results they want. One of the major keys to success is to *make the commitment to do what works* in terms of reaching your goals, instead of doing what *feels* pleasant in the short term.

> A young man who, like many others, grew up in a less-than-optimal environment: His father was highly narcissistic and an angry drunk, and his mother retreated into inner fantasy.
>
> For many years he thought that the way his parents acted and the way he felt about it, although unpleasant, was normal. Many years later he found out that it wasn't normal after all. As he was learning to do many new things and trying out new perspectives to overcome his upbringing, he realized that new things, and most often the very *things that work*...the *solutions*, don't feel normal. They feel *different*. And he was trained to believe, like so many others, that being *different* was bad, wrong and not-*ok*. All it took was one of *those* looks from a parent or respected person, or one of those comments, and he just *felt it*. Over time the meaning of "bad" became attached to the feeling of *different*. Even though he "knew" this, it was necessary to learn how to *overcome the feelings from these old bio-neurological structures*. Humans are faithful to old structures. *Where is your* **fidelity**?

In a similar way, new and healthier behaviors and habits at first feel alien. This is because they do not match the biochemical reality models and neuro-cortical pathways that currently exist in the brain. Remember, these structures are real and have substance, and like any other

substance can be changed and altered once you realize
what tools to use.

> Tense your body for a moment. You might begin to look at
> things that feel alien in a new light. Many people have a
> fascination with aliens and UFOs because the idea that there
> is something else out there—more advanced, different—
> opens up new possibilities. Why? Not because aliens are
> green or gray, but because they travel fast and go to new
> places, and *have greater abilities than the average human.*
> *Why is your greatest potential alien? Who and what are you*
> *being faithful to NOW?*

At first the brain attempts to reject the new behavior or
habit. This has been called "resistance" by psychoanalysts.
However, the word resistance has very negative connota-
tions for many individuals. What the brain is doing is
nothing more than **what it was designed to do**.

It holds on to habits, patterns and behaviors which
once worked—even though these patterns are no longer
useful.

The brain is so creative that it will attempt to prove
that the dangers and situations that were present at the
time of the creation of these patterns and behaviors still
exist. In other words, the brain gets off on hallucinating.

You already know that it can be difficult to differentiate when you are responding to subjective imagination or
external reality.

How do you experience this in your self?

Through feelings.

Feelings are communications to you from other parts
of you. Feelings *feel* like they are true—that is their nature.
In fact, most people believe that their feelings "make" their
beliefs true. Is that true?

A young boy is goofing around in the science room after school. Somehow, he gets the cord from the human skeleton display model (equipped with wheels for easy handling) hooked to his belt. He runs terrified down the street, screaming, as the skeleton chases him relentlessly toward certain doom. He crashes into a bush, his lifeless skeleton nemesis beside him...and then realizes that it was never a threat to him at all...

Is there any way, as he was running down the street, that the boy would believe you if you told him he had nothing to worry about? What would it take for him to be able to *stop,* turn to *face that skeleton,* and know that *you and you alone have the power to make it all right.*

Think about the skeleton story. Emotion and feelings didn't make it real...**and...**

These erroneous belief-feeling-identity loops have been called "self-fulfilling prophecies." The brain is designed to help you survive and it must first be convinced that its current pattern is being replaced with something better before is will let it go.

Go look in the mirror. What you see is the result of your beliefs-feelings-identity loops conveying to the world what you appear to be...whether people are conscious of what they see or not we all respond in one way or another to the illusions we see...... If you would like to change your illusion for a moment or two......jump up and down on a carpet for five minutes, twisting your face into different forms and pretending to laugh as hard as you can...... When your time is up, do it again for another five minutes if you wish, now go look into the mirror and see how interesting this new illusion is. Your new illusion will remain with you for about 20 minutes, maybe a little longer...... If you do this every day and go deeper as you jump higher, you will find newer and more interesting illusions.

In many ways it is easier to learn new skills that do not have strong emotional ties. Although we learn every day throughout our life, learning becomes more difficult when the new skill or behavior is related to a deeper emotional structure. In these cases, especially when the autonomic nervous system (ANS) becomes involved, deep fears and anxieties emerge that can be difficult to ignore. Emotion is like the mortar that holds the bricks together. The level of emotion is the measure of importance and is related to what is relevant for survival. At one time these strong emotions helped us cope, yet now they may be limiting and debilitating.

> Emotion simply marks out to the brain what to pay attention to. The 27-year-old woman knows that emotion and feelings are what "proves" that oranges are bad and that she cannot try new things, even though she now knows that there is no "logical" reason for this. She is *now* beginning to *realize that* **those** *feelings come from her lower brain, and not from data taken in by her senses.*

Realize that many so-called problems and limitations are nothing more than illusions and hallucinations made "real" by the emotions that are triggered to protect you. *Remember this* if and when those old feelings pop up when you begin to *think and do things differently—NOW—*

Chapter 5

Why Most Therapy Doesn't Work

The reason why most (but not all) therapy does not work is that therapists themselves have gotten into habits and belief systems which were at one time useful for them. Even though the models and belief systems may have been useful *in some contexts*, they are often incorporated into the therapist's own identity and color the "NOW" to such a degree that the patient is lost in the therapist's own learning structures.

In other words, most therapists and therapies do not view the patient as a naturalistic living process, but as a fixed thing with symptoms that needs to be fixed.

The therapist—by his very effort to become a therapist—has created a therapeutic hallucination which he has identified with.

Science Alert: In the field of physics, it is widely known and accepted that nothing is fixed, and that everything is constantly moving and changing. At the atomic level, the atoms themselves are mostly empty space, and the components that make up the protons, neutrons and electrons (superstring theory) are suspected to possibly not even exist. It seems to be that nothing is set in stone, even the stones themselves.

The term "patient" in and of itself describes a model and an attitude that attempts to dissociate the symptom from a natural living breathing entity.

This is called the *medical model*. This model is about being broken and needing to be fixed. This might be a useful way to look at cars. You already know that the map is not the territory, that *you are not the label*. People, on the other hand, *learn* limitations and difficulties, and do so often because that was the best thing to do, *at some time and place* **in the past.** It is important to *realize that what was learned can be* **unlearned**.

It is interesting to note that the word "fixed" means "locked in place" and "having been made all better" and at the same time…it just may be, that *fixing* is not what is needed at all.

> At one time, you may have believed in Santa Claus or the Tooth Fairy. And then you unbelieved it? It always feels so wonderful when I see that my clients all of a sudden *realize that all of your old problems and difficulties are just the same…and can also be unbelieved.*

Most therapies attempt to fit the patient into a particular pattern or box for the sake of the therapist's system.

Whether the system is Freudian, Jungian, Reichian, Rational-Emotive, Cognitive or whatever else is available, the patient becomes the victim of a model. Most therapists forget what the patient has come in for. He is unhappy and he is in pain. Thus, the job of the therapist is to assist the patient's creative self to heal himself and not to validate or support some theory or ideology (map).

The model, theory, map, hallucination or ideology exists *solely to assist the client*. The client does not exist to prove the theory or model. Many therapists and academics have completely forgotten this. Does the road exist for the cars or do the cars exist for the road? If someone told you that books exist so trees could be cut down, what would you say?

If the therapist is unable to assist in this process it is unacceptable behavior for them to continue treating a client. I know one therapist who has had the same patient for 16 years and the therapist's claim is that the patient had a major breakthrough: "He finally understood his anima projection." This is stupidity on the therapist's part—if not outright criminal.

> *You should expect and demand insight and skill from those who are assisting you in your personal evolution.*

This is no different than a physician who treats a patient with chemicals when a less dangerous remedy can be found.

The physician has been taught to believe only in drugs and, as a result, his identity and value become easily threatened by a healer who holds to a drugless therapy. I am not picking on physicians alone, for almost every type of healer I have met is a true believer in his own support system. Remember, each form of treatment rigorously attempts to stuff the natural process into conceptual frameworks created by the educational process the professional has undergone. It is good to know that even counselors and psychologists (*you* know who *you* are) *can unbelieve yourself right out of a rigid and inflexible approach.* It is as simple as not pouring the water down the drain with the spaghetti it was cooked in.

> Even though your conscious mind has recognized the illusion in the last sentence and you may have repeated the expected sequence of words to yourself...your unconscious mind has corrected the "broken" expectation—that it is not the water but the spaghetti. If this is true, tap once with your happy finger, the one you like the best; if not, take three deep breaths. Can you explain to a stranger that *believing is seeing*?

> Therapeutic theory and models are best attempts at provid-
> ing an understanding for how things work and for providing
> a map for change.
>   But *remember that the map is not the territory.* An archi-
> tect can have plans of a house and show them to his client.
> He really has no idea how the client feels inside his current
> abode or how he will feel inside when he finally arrives at his
> new home—or does he? You decide. BUT WAIT—I have pro-
> vided you with only two options—how many more are
> there?

That healers may be rigid True Believers should not discourage anyone from seeking treatment. However, what should be kept in mind is that *you* are THE authority in deciding which way to go and how creative you would like to be in finding solutions.

Your internal support system has worked for you in the past and will be sure to work in the future. Over the past two decades some researchers have learned much about how the brain and nervous system operate. They have come forward with new methods to help individuals use their creative resources to remove and replace beliefs and behavior which are no longer of any real use. This non-book and the methods contained within are simply new tools to assist nature in her goal of perfecting her most interesting hallucination—you.

Chapter 6

Multiple Levels

You have a part of you that keeps your heart beating, keeps you breathing, blinks your eyes and digests your food—all without your having to think about it.

These parts of you operate at different levels of awareness, and most often not in your "normal" level of (word-label) consciousness.

These parts of you have commonly been labeled your unconscious mind, your subconscious mind and your other-than-conscious mind. No matter what you call it, you can think of yourself as having multiple levels. Whether any of these concepts are "true" or not, it can be useful to think of it this way for the sake of self-understanding.

Throughout the self-discovery process you will become increasingly aware that you are a multi-level communicator who can be as clear as necessary. You will also learn that you do not have to be clear at one level of communication to be clear at another. You can *be comfortable* and *trust all levels of yourself,* the very same way you trust a certain part of yourself to keep your heart beating. "Hasn't skipped a beat" is a high compliment for anything technical, mechanical and for yourself, *so you can relax now and trust yourself,* because these parts of you are looking out for you and taking care of things you normally aren't aware of.

Realizing this will speed up your progress as you don't have to understand exactly what is happening and how it is happening for you to *utilize it fully and benefit from it **now***, allowing you to move more quickly. If you had to learn medicine to benefit from undergoing surgery, you would have to wait many years until you finished medical school. You have probably already waited long enough, and *you no longer need any extra weight anymore.*

Many solutions are simply one or two steps removed from conscious awareness. Your job is to continue your own development while, at the same time, being confident that any necessary re-structuring is also taking place at those levels.

Most of your thinking and re-evaluation of the past and future takes place out of awareness. Do you believe this or do you know this? Many people don't think that they are thinking without awareness. How about you? Do you know that 99% of what is going on is doing so without your conscious consent? Some people are horrified at this prospect... How do you think about not thinking with your consent? Remember, what you see on the screen of your mind, like the screen of a computer, is not what is going on behind the scenes.

Keep in mind that for many people consciousness means they are aware of "verbal" thoughts—sometimes called subvocal thinking—going through their minds. This gives them the illusion that they are in charge and have control over what is going on.

It is easy to learn without the conscious realization that we are learning. In fact, you have been doing just that this whole time, haven't you?

Have you ever wondered why in many cases you do much better than you expect? Knowledge and change are not always dependent on verbal understanding. Remember the story about the young boy who was able to perform well on a test without having conscious verbal recall.

We assume that a person is intelligent if he can verbalize what he can access from his memory. Both the ability to recall and the ability to verbalize are skills with a high interpersonal value.

Also highly valued is the ability to organize what you recall and verbalize. Although this skill is not an ultimate test of knowledge or intelligence, individuals who can verbalize and organize the information they recall are considered smart. They frequently get ahead of those individuals whose actual Intelligence Quotients are significantly higher. Why is this? In the Western world our perception of intelligence is often based on the ability to verbalize and regurgitate information—regardless of whether it is understood or can be applied.

> Consider a military historian and strategist. This intellectual most likely has stored an enormous amount of information: dates, facts and scenarios. He also will be able to produce this information through writing papers, articles and books, as well as through extensive lectures. Yet, this does not mean he has any ability in any form of combat in the field. In fact, most soldiers and operatives have little respect for these people, because their information is based only on verbal recall, instead of from *actually doing it.*

> Remember that real understanding and ability often require a muscular memory component and not simply an intellectual "understanding." Many successful people *rehearse the motions required to accomplish a task in their mind's eye* long before they attempt it.

Many individuals severely limit themselves from improving their lives because they only evaluate themselves on their ability to recall, organize and verbalize information and somehow forget their other abilities and successes. If this has ever been you, remember the soldiers who **make things happen** *without ever worrying* about their verbal skills.

You may also be pleasantly surprised that as your self-understanding increases along with the other changes you are making, your ability to communicate verbally also increases.

Another very important thing that we know: most mind-body communication is non-verbal.

This explains why simple positive thinking is not sufficient to cause radical or permanent change in the short term. Positive thinking is not thinking at all, it is simply thoughting.

Positive thinking does have its place. You remember that a part of your mind responds powerfully to your internal subjective experience. Therefore it makes sense to *use your ability to think and to imagine, to picture **what you want***. This would be better called positive imagining—which would involve more than a thought or a wish but rather a complete picture.

Most individuals have conflicted feelings about certain issues.

This is sometimes reflected in the contradiction between verbal and non-verbal responses. The most obvious is saying **yes** while moving the head ever-so-slightly to indicate **no**. This is called incongruency, and researchers have long known that these non-verbal reactions often indicate deeper attitudes and structures. These structures are usually out of conscious awareness and control, and often sabotage conscious intention. This should shine some light on why it is so easy to make promises to yourself and more difficult to keep them.

When there is a conflict between levels, the level that wins out is usually the one that is closest to the emotional centers of the brain.

To repeat:

When there is a conflict between levels, the level that wins out is usually the one that is closest to the emotional centers of the brain.

How might this work? Say you decide to lose weight. You are not fully aware that at times being overweight brought you attention...and that you liked the attention, even if it were negative attention. So now you start the diet and drop 10 pounds, but in two weeks find that you gained 15 pounds. *This is a result of conflicting levels of intention and desire, so unless you get down there and UNDO it, your conscious intention will be overridden by the deeper levels.* If you wish to UNDO your deeper levels, tap twice with your favorite finger; if you don't wish to UNDO your deeper levels, smile and shake your head yes.

The concepts that are learned and programmed at different levels may be in conflict. We can return to the earlier example, where a young child learns that it is useful to play stupid to be accepted and to survive within the family. Survival will almost always supersede a skill like organization or punctuality. Your higher rational brain clearly understands that *being organized and on time is useful,* yet the lower brain, which was imprinted and developed first, has more influence on how you *feel.* Even though you know that you would be more successful if organized, the part of you that is "taking care of survival" *has a different perception of how to be successful—the old pattern.*

Through the methods of deeper level holistic communication that you are now learning, *appropriate changes can now take place* allowing you to resolve these conflicts.

Verbal communication alone is not sufficient to cause change and, in many instances, is unnecessary. Getting in touch with one's feelings and beginning to use them as information is also important. This is often referred to as emotional intelligence, instinct and gut feeling.

It is important to be able to differentiate instinct from rumination. Rumination is the random thinking that goes round and round inside your mind, in your subjective reality. Most people do not distinguish between the emotions that are caused by rumination and the feelings they have from external reality.

When your brain is ruminating, you can rest assured that some deeper emotion is driving the thoughts. If you stop the ruminating for a moment, look around your mind, and ask it what the conflict is, you may receive an answer. When you translate the answer into simple language you may see that you are conflicted: angry, fearful or something similar.

There are many reasons why you ruminate, but here's one of the most important: you believe that if you realize an emotion fully, you must act on it (and most of these kind of emotions which would lead to action could have been dangerous to your survival at one time and might even be dangerous now). What you need to realize is that emotion doesn't mean YOU HAVE TO ACT on it. Children have a hard time realizing this, so they suppress or repress their emotions as they mature, however those emotions still exist at a deeper level, and in adults often express themselves as ruminations.

How do you learn to distinguish instinct from rumination? You *watch and practice.* You learn about how you work; then, when things are happening you can *stop yourself and remember what is going on.*

You also need to accept your feelings—not make them illegal—and honor that communication. Using your rationality and figuring out where they come from, you will be able to stop them before they get too big. They are like a fire alarm. Train your attention so IT doesn't get stuck on it, and IT can be pointed toward the process and what you really want.

From this point now you are informed and can begin to use your rational mind to make better decisions. This is why you have been reading about perception, the construction of meaning, and brain functioning when you may not been expecting to.

You will often notice that when you do *stop in real time and* **use your new information to make new decisions, you will have new and different feelings instead of the old ones.** As you remember that *feeling different is ok,* you may find that the new feelings that begin building are the long-awaited ones such as personal power, relief, freedom, joy and self-esteem.

Verbal communication is not the language of habit or the language of the body.

Every thought causes a reaction in the body and every body-reaction and sensation creates thought. These thoughts may not make any sense to you—at least not to your conscious mind.

Consider how many interesting but "random" thoughts you have each day. Each one is connected to a set of belief patterns that for some (unpleasant) reason you prefer to forget.

One solution is to try to remember—but if nothing comes, then do something quite different. One way to effect change (and communicate with your deeper levels) is to engage in behaviors that run contrary to your feelings. Have some fun even if you are unhappy and see what happens. When you are sad, put on some fun music and dance. Smile with all of your might for two minutes or pretend to laugh. A "random" thought or emotion may tell you a lot.

Behavioral experimentation is a great way to communicate to your deeper levels that change is desired. It is important to first differentiate between subjective and objective reality. Walking along the ledge of a tall building *should* create some fear and anxiety. That is the useful function of fear. Having this fear when stepping off a curb may be somewhat excessive. In this case, talking and talking about your fear will probably not do much for you (or others). But *doing* something different—like practicing stepping off a curb in a safe place 25 times a day—will create a non-verbal learning.

> As you think of some of the things you would like to change about yourself, you may begin to think of new things you would like to try. These will be the types of actions that you *know* would be beneficial to you, yet in the past may have only felt uncomfortable. These can be your behavior experiments. Write these ideas down in your notebook.

You may want to try these out in real life; or a part of you might do this when you dream; or while you are listening to the companion CDs and DVDs; or all of them.

Many people have found that some of the things they learn as they heal and evolve are not new, but *remembered*. It's as if a part of you has known all along that *deep down you are just fine,* and upon realizing this wondered how you could have forgotten this in the first place. Could this be your *fidelity* to an unhappy person of your past? Sometimes people refuse to be happy because...? Do you really have to be faithful to your past?

Our ability to think and imagine can create problems in and of itself. We must constantly strive to **remember** *that* our subjective **reality** *is our own creation.*

When we create disasters, monsters and worst-case scenarios inside our mind, the rest of us responds accordingly, and then we experience the feelings that prove it.

To repeat:

When we create disasters, monsters and worst-case scenarios inside our mind, the rest of us responds accordingly, and then we experience the feelings that prove it.

Often you will see this when talking to someone and notice that the problem they are having has been solved by the information you have given them—but they still continue complaining and ruminating. At that time you must realize that they are possessed, as if by a demon. What do you do? Either do nothing and watch; or, if you dare, pinch them. Often a mild shock can move a person out of this painful circle.

I would have clients run around the block until they were exhausted and then allow them to *go deeper and deeper until the demon would be exorcised.*

Once our psycho-physiology is going in that direction, it influences our ability to concentrate, our ability to recall and our motor skills. This in turn creates objective "proof" that our initial "belief" is true, thus creating a self-fulfilling prophecy. Why are self-fulfilling prophecies self-fulfilling?

A young man prepares to give a talk to a large audience for the first time.

Inside his mind he pictures the audience staring at him with bored and disapproving scowls. Inside his mind he hears their comments about how terrible he is. By the time he reaches the podium, his heart rate has increased, his blood pressure has risen and adrenaline is flowing. As he starts to speak, he has difficulty remembering the name of the person who introduced him, and his internal dialogue starts to berate him. Soon he starts fumbling his papers and drops them on the floor, which further become "evidence" of his inability.

He barely makes it through, and decides that he is a terrible public speaker.

This is the common self-fulfilling prophecy. The solution is to catch the process as soon as you can, and change it around to the way you want it to be.

One way to change it is through imagining. Begin to picture inside your mind what you want, use your internal dialogue to reinforce it, and generate the feelings that you want. After all, it is your mind, and you can use it however you want.

It takes the same amount of energy to imagine success as it does failure. (Every time you imagine failure once you may imagine success twice—*do it now.*)

The young man in the story above can also picture the audience nodding in agreement and smiling, and then giving a standing ovation.

He could picture himself behaving in a powerful and graceful manner, as he hears the compliments and praise of his audience.

Since these internal processes influence your brain, nervous system and, thus, your outcomes, it makes sense to *start using your internal processes to contribute to your objectives*, doesn't it. Does it? Failure is often *fidelity*—

For some people, this is a startling *"AHA"*. Maybe you never thought of this before, and most likely no one ever told you that *you can do this*. So…now you know and can begin using your mind in a deliberate positive manner.

Another way to change self-fulfilling prophecies is through your behavior; this is called "acting as if."

At this point many clients violently object. They say that "acting as if" is not "real" or "genuine." **(But *fidelity* to failure is?)**

After all, how can you act one way and feel another? The answer is, *you just do it.* (Hey, who says you can't?) The person you have been—your traditional and habitual self—is no more real than any other self you could be. The only thing that makes it seem real is…your feeling—habits. (*Yes, most feelings are simply habits.*)

You decide.

You set the direction, because if you don't, then you will simply be following the dictates of your old beliefs and patterns, which were set in place before you were smart enough or had enough rational and perceptual ability to realize that they were grossly inaccurate. If you don't *decide for yourself*, then you will remain "stuck."

The implications of this are staggering.

Your ability to "imagine" that you have a problem will send you on a mission to "fix" it.

Your ability to declare yourself "not ok" will send you on a journey to get back to "ok." You can replace "not ok" with "not good enough," "worthless," "undeserving," or whatever you prefer.

The problem is only a problem because you created it and labeled it in your mind—and then forgot that you did this. Thus, *the problem exists only in your perception* that something about you is inherently wrong, bad or broken.

If *the problem exists* only in your subjective evaluation—*only in your thinking*—then the journey toward fixing this problem—the destination of "ok" or "good enough"—is based on the presupposition that something is inherently "wrong." This is the type of problem that can never be solved and is the destination that can never be reached. If you are searching and struggling to find your way to the destination "ok", you cannot reach it, because you never left it. And a part of you, deep down, knows that this is so. I call the realization and experience of this "coming home" or, sometimes, creative in*fidelity*.

Chapter 7

Every Behavior Has Served A Useful Purpose

Every *self-defeating* behavior and belief has at one time or another served a **useful purpose**. It is good to stop for a moment and let this sink in. Every behavior was, at one time and place, *in your best estimate* **at that time,** set up for a useful purpose. Every belief was formed, at one time and place, with the best of your ability to perceive and attach meaning to those events, to serve a **useful purpose—AT THAT TIME!**

Behind the useful purpose is a very noble intention: *you were operating in* **your own best interest** *with the resources you had at the time to* **protect yourself and meet your own needs.**

The difference between **NOW** and then is that *NOW you have more options.* You have gained more knowledge, insight and experience since then. Your brain has developed more. Your willingness to be curious, although latent, is curiously stronger.

Right now is the best time to re-explore old beliefs, ideas and concepts because you have never been older or more experienced or more insightful than you are right now. You can decide for yourself *now* if the old limiting behaviors and beliefs are the ones that you want, or that they can use some updating.

There are causal chains that are **NOW** untrue, although at one time they *felt like* they were true and *appeared* to be useful.

Most early causal chains are manufactured by the creative functions of the early mind. The important thing to remember is that there is a difference between *unacceptable behavior* and a **useful purpose.**

Smoking, for example, may have served the purpose of reducing tension, allowing you to do otherwise stressful things. It may have made you feel socially acceptable at one time, or may have been an indicator of becoming a adult. While the behavior of smoking has **now** become *unacceptable* to **you,** reducing stress, being socially accepted and being an adult are still **useful** and **desirable**. The important thing **now** is to reduce stress and improve social interaction with more useful and personally acceptable behaviors. Do you see how these neural bond chains keep you faithful? You might call this creative *fidelity*; however, NOW it is stale.

The funny thing about some deeper analytical levels is that they are time-bound (fixed like concrete in time) and are not aware of deeper changes that have taken place, or of the new possibilities. While many of the goals are the same, the behaviors and thought sequences created back then often are no longer useful and sometimes limiting.

> Time-bound material is literally fixed at the time it was cre-
> ated and often feels like it is the "real" you... You may find a
> challenge here......the time-bound material may not want
> to be brought up to the present—you will know this when a
> lot of anxiety is present. In this sense, anxiety is useful since it
> provides you with important information. **What do you do?**
> *Invoke a most pleasant memory and attach it to the anxiety...*
> If you do this a number of times, pleasure will take the place
> of anxiety and you will be surprised—the time-bound
> material will leap forward to the present and, if you desire,
> *you can consciously update the material.*

An example is a woman who had great difficulties in
experiencing pleasure while having sex. She remembered
that when she was 12 her mother told her that sex was
dangerous and evil. The purpose behind this communication was to protect her from pregnancy and social rejection
from peers.

But in the mother's attempt to protect her, she forget to
communicate that what she said was useful only while her
daughter was young and vulnerable, and not when she
was older and more capable of discrimination. Remember:
past useful information and behaviors are always time and
space bound.

Fifteen years later, the daughter's body was still react-
ing with rigidity and tension prior to and during inter-
course with her husband. She was also having great difficulty getting pregnant.

The woman sought treatment. Once she realized that
her mother's communication was temporal (time-space
bound) she began to relax and got pregnant easily. She
was able to realize the useful purpose of the communication, which was to keep her safe by avoiding behavior
inappropriate *for a 12-year-old.* She realized that there are
other, more appropriate ways to keep safe besides absti-
nence, avoidance and guilt. But this girl-woman was faithful to her time-bound messages as well as to the image of
her "mother" as omnipotent.

What this means to you is that you can *choose to give up* your s*elf-defeating behavior* **now** without giving up the useful purpose.

To repeat:

What this means to you is that you can choose to give up your self-defeating behavior now without giving up the useful purpose.

This way, you won't have to worry about internal conflicts. *Resistance to change comes from the part of you that is holding onto the useful purpose, but is not yet convinced that the new behavior will satisfy that purpose.* Once you fully realize this, you can easily decide what behaviors you can begin letting go of, and what new behaviors you can put in their place—behaviors that meet your useful purposes even better.

The important thing to remember is that there is a difference between *unacceptable behavior* and a **useful purpose.**

You might choose to think of things like excessive emotional reactions—fear and anxiety, procrastination and co-dependency—as *behaviors,* as things that you are *doing,* instead of things that always "just happen" to you. By developing the perspective that these reactions are not external or random will allow you to *gain control over them and replace them with more suitable ones.*

To repeat:

What this means to you is that you can choose to give up *your* self-defeating behavior now *without giving up the useful purpose (which hides behind the behaviors).*

It is very common to think that behavioral and emotional reactions are "caused" by things outside of your control, things such as situational and environmental factors and, especially, other people. This belief only acts as a shield. If other things and people are doing things to you, then it is not your fault and not your responsibility. This may *seem* to remove you from the equation, but you are the one who ends up suffering. The flip side to this is that your response is not under your control, and you become a victim of it *and* of the factors and people who "cause" you to respond, react and feel the way you do.

Guilt and Other Intrusive Monsters:
Behind every guilt feeling there are beliefs—yes, not just one or two but many... Put this non-book down for a moment or two, don't go deep, just touch the surface and feel. Sooner or later some beliefs will pop up and then you can analyze them critically. In another chapter you will find energized exercises that will bring forth hidden beliefs, thoughts and feelings. You might jump to that now—or simply continue on—

There are two common behavioral patterns people develop to combat their perceived lack of control. One is to become the aggressor and attempt to dominate oneself, others and the environment.

This entails forcing yourself, others and your environment to conform to your conscious desires. Most often this attempt results in your being brought to your knees and humbled by those factors which will not succumb to your efforts. This then requires a more outrageous version of the faulty response to regain your position on top, thus reinforcing the problematic patterns and beliefs.

The other common pattern is to become a victim of your past experiences, your situation, or other people—or all of the above.

Sooner or later you will become a terminal victim, believing that you have absolutely no power or ability to change yourself or your circumstances.

This response becomes self-fulfilling very quickly, and creates plenty of evidence that reinforces these patterns and beliefs. You also tend to end up under the feet of those who have the aggressor's response.

Either response is ineffectual and limiting, and continues to reinforce the painful and limiting beliefs and patterns that are holding you back. I imagine that you can find in your memory a few people who remind you of these incomplete perceptions of how things work......

There are also many stories of people who have started out as victims and then used that awareness to create extraordinary lives for themselves, overcoming all odds. Dave Pelzer, author of *A Child Called IT*, is one example. It is highly likely that you can find someone who has had a similar experience to yours, and who was able to *decide to evolve anyway*.

More often than not you will find mixed types who switch between the aggressor and the victim. This type has sometimes been referred to as being "either at your throat or at your feet." Can you name a few people like this?

While it is true that external factors may serve as the trigger, and may have been the reason you developed the patterns and beliefs in the first place, your patterns are still your own creation, and your reactions are still your own *doing*. It may not be your "fault" but now it is *your* responsibility. It is up to *you* to *decide which things are no longer serving you and drop them*. The good news is, *you are free to change your style at any time. Or is being faithful to failure that important for—?*

You may not like the carpeting in your home. It may be old, dirty and an odd color.

It may have been there as long as you can remember. Most likely you don't want anyone else to see it either.

When you actually think about it, it might even "make" you feel bad.

But, don't stop there.

Remember that *you can change it.*

The solution is to begin to become aware of your limiting beliefs, behaviors and patterns. Acknowledge and take full responsibility for them. *Let yourself off the hook, stop judging yourself* and choose more suitable ones that allow yourself to reach your goals and live the life that you really want.

It is good to remember that *you are not your behavior,* and since *you are not your past* or present behavior, *you* can *redesign your behaviors to suit your current needs.* After all, right now *is* the best time, isn't it or maybe not—maybe yesterday was better, but what about tomorrow?

If yesterday was better than tomorrow and today was worse then yesterday, what are you going to do NOW?

As you read along and use the CDs and DVDs, you will have the opportunity to explore this further and *begin to make adjustments.* As new thoughts and ideas begin to come to you, write them down.

You might look at it as a loop: you change the environment and the environment changes you. Remember that *you* are the part of the equation that you have the most control and influence over. By changing yourself *first*, your environment will begin to change as well. Also remember that we have more influence over external and situational factors than we are used to imagining, and you can learn to have even more—because you have already, haven't you.

To repeat:

What this means to you is that you can **choose to give up** *your* **self-defeating** *behavior* now *without giving up the useful purpose. But what about yesterday, when it was better?*

As you begin to develop new associations and beliefs and construct new behaviors, you will, from time to time, become aware of the less useful response re-appearing. This is **not** a sign that it is not working or that you are not learning. It is a natural part of the process of change. When the old behavior appears, simply observe it and be respectful. Do not judge it or in any other way be cruel to it. Just as you have learned to watch your feelings, simply watch. In a moment or two it will recede into the background as it continues to undergo constructive re-formulation.

As you gain more experience, your sense of power will increase. Whether you wish to change a belief or a behavior, engage it at its own level of communication—*and always remember to be respectful to yourself*—even to your most hideous qualities. This was one of the major secrets of the ancients......

Self-change does not follow easily after self-depreca-tion and in a climate of self-hate. You want to cooperate with those parts of you, and you want their cooperation. Since some of your most powerful and emotional learnings were acquired before the age of 7, we urge you to *treat yourself with the respect, kindness and understanding you would show a young child who is learning something new, or who is upset about something that has happened to them.*

Chapter 8

The Learning Perspective

You are a learning machine. It is the nature of the organism. The goal of learning is just that...*learning*. The goal of learning (or any new endeavor for that matter) is **not** perfection on the first try, but continued evaluation and improvement. This is why it is important to *be kind to yourself as you evaluate and learn*. If you aren't, learning can be emotionally painful—which is why most people never do it, and which is why most people remain stuck for their entire lives. (*How faithful are you to success?*) They didn't *learn how to learn*—which is how to do self-analysis—and *find out what worked and what didn't*, and then *make the appropriate changes and adjustments as you go*. Leave your value as a human being and your self-worth alone (just leave it at 100%). *Remember, for every negative self-statement, you may do two positive self-acts.*

You might be wondering why there is so much emphasis on *learning*. Learning is a process. We are a process, and a work in progress. Nothing in this universe is static.

It is all always moving, always changing. The important difference is that none of these atomic particles and structures feel bad about this. Only humans do this. (***How much faith do you have in feeling bad?***)

This brings us to a very important discussion, so *pay close attention.*

Through many years of study and experience, I have found something very curious. While it is no secret, it is so obvious that many have simply missed it.

Those people who have a bad time at life seem to be "metaphysical generalizers." (See *The Black Book* by C.S. Hyatt.) It seems as though success in life is inversely proportional to the amount of metaphysical generalizing one does.

Metaphysical generalizing refers to the process of observing the actions and behaviors of your self and then assigning a value judgment and label to it. Once this process is started and believed in, it becomes what is often referred to as self-fulfilling prophecy.

Metaphysical generalizers put things into broad, global categories:

1. I am fundamentally good (worthy).
2. I am fundamentally no good (worthless).
3. I sometimes am good and sometimes no good.

Which then leads to the external world:

1. Others are fundamentally good.
2. Others are fundamentally no good.
3. Sometimes others are good and sometimes no good.

That makes the stakes pretty high, doesn't it.

If in everything I do, I am playing for the absolute value and worth of my self as an individual human being... No wonder people hesitate, avoid, procrastinate, fall short and feel anxious.

We are constantly torn between our factual existence and our infinite capacity to imagine and fantasize. Or, one might say, torn between our objective reality and subjective reality. Just because we can label something doesn't make the label "true" of us.

Science alert: In the field of physics, they have discovered that the characteristics and properties of an observed entity do not exist in the entity itself, but in the perception of the observer. Example: One would normally say "the ball is red." A physicist would say "the ball appears to reflect the red spectrum of light under certain conditions in a specific time and place." The quality of "redness" is not *in* the ball, but based on the perception of the observer. (Be careful not to turn this observation into metapuke.)

So what, you may ask. You may not even like science (or didn't think you did). **But,** if you take what is known from science, and apply it to yourself, you end up with something very valuable.

It means that the labels you have given yourself (and the labels others have given you and which you agreed to) are not "in you," but are in your perception of yourself. **SO, that means that all of the "labels"—like bad, wrong, stupid, lazy, dumb, failure, no-good, worthless, and anything else—are not "you."**

SO Sorry, to those of you who think that negativity, depression, big words, and things that go bumpy in the night imply truth......

A simple example: remember when you were a young child, and another child called you a "picklehead," and you ran in the house and looked in the mirror, you saw that there was no pickle there (although you may have imagined it so on the way inside). How is that any different than those other things that you have said about yourself?

So what then "makes" something true? We have discussed earlier that our "feelings" do not make things true, and now we are saying that "language" and labeling do not make things "true" either.

As you will notice, these strange and curious thoughts and ideas are circular and self-perpetuating. For example, a person in trouble comes in for help. The fact that they are in trouble and the fact that they need help means...you guessed it.

These are *exactly* the types of *meanings* and *beliefs* that are formed when we are young, when the mind is not fully developed.

> It is a common initial reaction to completely deny that there is any possibility that **"you"** *might have some of these kinds of limiting beliefs.* I call this the "look under that rock again" phenomenon. When you are absolutely sure that you know that something isn't "true" for or about you, you will probably find "the answer" by looking there again.

Recap: Don't assign global value judgments to yourself as you are learning.

(Hey guys—a truly worthless person wouldn't be concerned about being worthless. Or, who is this **I** that says **I** am good or no good? How do you feel about this **I**? Who in the hell is she anyway?) Who are you more faithful to, mommy or daddy?

When you free yourself from this nonsense, you will literally be able to do anything you wish, as long as you are passionate about it and seek to learn as much as you can...!!!

In contrast to **Metaphysical Generalizers**, I have noticed another curious type of person. For this person, fundamental or metaphysical conclusions are not an issue. They are not relevant. He is a "Here I Am Person." He simply *experiences* events and situations, and if he generalizes, he does so from his observations. He doesn't need to know the "Great" answers. When he has answers, he has them. He likes events, experiences and things. He takes interest in things that interest him. His sense of his basic self is non-comparative. This means he uses comparison to learn, instead of for self-evaluation and judgment.

The identity of this person is the "Natural Child" who is unassisted by the need to discuss their own self-worth.

They *realize that worth is not a relevant issue, and cannot be*. Have you ever heard of a fetus considering its worth for life before propelling itself into life?

> Is it possible to be "wrong" or "bad" as a human being—at the level of mere existence? **NO.** How would one measure this? It is always done by *feelings*. The single most devastating error a young mind makes is adopting the fictitious belief that *since I feel bad, I must be bad*. But this does not prove that it is even *possible* to be bad, or wrong, or worthless. It simply shows us that we *have the power to create* a concept, forget that **we** did it, and then become imprisoned in our own creation. Do you remember when you did this last?

If you have to *decide* if you are fundamentally good and worthy of life, then you're open to a world of misery—because your mental decision *implies that it is true*. Example: If I ask you if you have ever seen a blue elephant, the question presupposes that they exist. **Most people never question the validity of the concepts they are imprisoned by.** Even if you decide that you are good and worthy of life, your decision is open to re-decision because it was up for question to begin with. The solution: *begin to question "truth."*

> The last paragraph in a box contains one of the greatest **frauds** ever pulled on us. It is the way in which people are manipulated and controlled by those in "authority" over us. That means parents, religions, politics, and all other entities that have a lock on "the truth." It is worth your time to *carefully consider and understand this.*

The natural person, unassisted by fundamental metaphysical evaluations, is not vulnerable to such judgments and re-evaluations since there were no primal evaluations to begin with. He is alive and needs to assume nothing. What assumptions are you faithful to?

Now, I am worried that some of you might begin to feel that you are fundamentally good or no-good. If you feel that way, don't be concerned because your work here will bring you back to your "unassisted self."

Just because we habitually think of ourselves in a certain way doesn't mean it's true. It is important to realize that *the part of your map that describes **yourself** is also not the territory. Your self-concept is not your self. The labels **were never you!** A part of you may have responded to those old useless labels and they **were never you!***

P.S.: Welcome home to the freedom of being your true self.

Tests, Exercises and Techniques

Chapter 9

Communicating At A Deeper Level

In the previous chapter you read about a woman who wanted to get pregnant, but a younger part of her was trying to protect her in ways that were conflicting with her adult goals and desires. Like her, you may find in yourself that the purpose or function of your behavior still has a positive intention for you *from its own perspective* **at the time it was created.** That part of you is probably on auto-pilot, and may not be communicating with you. One of your goals along the way will be to develop a relationship with that part of you.

> The idea of having parts is a metaphor for understanding yourself. *Remember the idea of mood modules,* which implies that our individual mood-states have different neurological circuits devoted to them. This also implies that the resources we have available to us at some times and places may not be available in others......***yet***.

The function of the lower brain is to protect the organism. This is accomplished through the emotions, which steered the organism (you) toward and away from certain things that *it perceived were nourishing or harmful...***at that time of development.**

So, keep in mind that even if some of these beliefs and behaviors are not useful now, that part of you is only doing the best job it can for you.

Earlier we discussed that smoking (for example) may have served the purpose of reducing tension, allowing you to do otherwise stressful things. It may have made you feel socially acceptable at one time or may have been an indicator of your becoming a adult. While *the behavior of smoking has now become unacceptable* to **you,** reducing stress, *being socially accepted and being an adult* are *still useful and desirable*. The important thing **now** is to reduce stress and improve social interaction with *more useful and acceptable behaviors*.

Other examples, although more painful, are the concepts of self-sabotage, the fear of success, procrastination, and the lack of follow-through. These may have served the purpose of providing security and protection in situations that were perceived as "bad" or "wrong."

When was yesterday? Which yesterdays are you faithful to? How many tomorrows are slipping away because of *fidelity* —so **NOW is not yesterday or tomorrow**. If you agree tap three times with NOW'S finger; if not slap yourself with yesterday's hand.

I once treated a patient who was very stubborn. He resisted any help I offered him to gain insight into his problems and change his behavior. His stubbornness took the shape of passiveness: saying **no** without having to say **no**. I asked him why such a behavior or habit would develop. The answer followed immediately as he drifted off into a light trance. He responded that if he said **no** directly there would be a horrible argument and he would be persuaded to do what his father wanted regardless of how distasteful it might be. Instead of saying no, he would agree and either forget or sulk in silence.

When he learned to argue better, he would say **no** to anything anyone would directly suggest, even if he knew at some level it would be good for him to follow through.

I suggested that he try to remember one or two situations where he said either **no** or **yes** and which did not lead to unpleasant results. I suggested that before he tried to remember these situations that he respond to my suggestion by lifting either arm if he agreed or by lifting the other arm if he disagreed. (Lifting of the arms is an example of multi-level communication.) For a moment nothing happened and then both arms lifted. I told him to proceed as he saw fit, if and only if he was ready to drop one arm. If he wasn't ready to proceed directly he could hold both arms out and move right along by passing over his need for verbal consent.

Without going into further detail, he learned to say no when it suited him, but only after he realized that saying **yes** or **no** brought out immense fears of punishment and desertion, created at a particular time and place when he had few other options to deal with his authoritarian father and his manipulative mother. Did he have *fidelity*?

Take break now and look at some sexy pictures. If you agree, raise both arms; if not raise your other arm.

Often the individual has no conscious awareness of these kinds of underlying beliefs.

What they are aware of is the frustration, pain and confusion that arises from wanting to move in a certain direction, and somehow being "held back" by unknown forces.

Remember those upcoming exercises. Should you use them now or use them soon, or have you used them? Who is in charge here?

The individual will often have an aggressive attitude toward these characteristics and, not realizing their positive intention, will try to "chase those parts away with a stick." It is no wonder why these parts do not generally communicate with you—and thus the need to begin to develop a better relationship with yourself.

I have often asked clients to get comfortable, close their eyes, and simply notice the feelings and emotions that correspond to their problem. I then ask them to *say hello* to that and to *welcome it*. This in itself usually produces a noticeable change, even after years of chasing it away. I then ask the client to *apologize* to it, for being angry at it, and then promise to acknowledge it from now on as a valuable asset and resource. Next, I ask the client to *ask that part of yourself to begin to communicate with you*, and then to ask the part that is attached to the feeling to tell you and show you what its positive intention has been.

Clients have almost fallen out of their chairs when their *fear of failure tells them it just wants you to remember that you can really do it.*

I have seen amazing relief and self-respect grow when their anxiety gives them the solutions to challenges in their lives.

You can do this on your own, and the above exercise will be helpful to you as you will be gathering some information about the useful purpose and beliefs behind your behaviors. *Be patient, warm and welcoming* to those feelings, and you will begin to *strengthen your relationship with yourself.*

Another method of communicating with yourself is called the body pendulum.

Stand in a quiet place, and ask your body to lean in the direction of **yes.** Then ask your body to lean in the direction of **no.** Once you have established yes and no, you can begin to validate this by asking specific yes or no questions, such as "Am I a boy?"

This is another method to elicit information from your other levels. You may even find yourself leaning slightly in situations with other people, and *find yourself making better decisions* that honor you more.

Still another method to communicate with deeper levels is to set up finger signals. In the hypnosis circle this is called "ideomotor communication." For example, you can decide that your right index finger is your **yes** finger, and your left index finger is your **no** finger. You can also do this with your right foot and left foot. In a very relaxed, meditative state, you simply *ask that deeper part of you that it is willing to communicate with you by moving the appropriate finger. (But you have been doing this all along without knowing everything about it.)*

Now, this may happen right away, or it might happen later while you listen to the CDs and DVDs. As you begin to trust those deeper levels, this becomes easier. You will notice that your finger will move somewhat differently than it does when directed by your conscious mind.

There is one last component of self communication we will explore here. The results of the following test will provide you with a greater understanding of yourself.

Take the following test, circle the letter that seems most familiar—most natural—to you.

1. As someone makes a statement you agree with, your response is:
   - A. I see what you mean
   - B. I hear what you're saying
   - C. That feels right to me
2. You are most attracted to:
   - A. Vivid colors
   - B. Certain music
   - C. Something soft and fuzzy
3. The phrase:
   - A. It's time to get focused
   - B. It's time to turn up the volume
   - C. It's time to turn up the heat
4. You just forgot something and:
   - A. It's hiding right in front of me
   - B. It's on the tip of my tongue
   - C. I can't put my finger on it
5. Something familiar:
   - A. Seems right
   - B. Rings a bell
   - C. Feels right
6. With a friend you like to:

       A. Be seen for who you are
       B. Be heard
       C. Be connected

7. When angry:
       A. Get out of my sight
       B. Shut up
       C. Get off my back

8. The scary part of a haunted house:
       A. What it looked like
       B. What you heard
       C. What you felt

9. When you are in love, you most think of:
       A. That certain look on your lover's face
       B. Certain things your lover says or the tone of their voice
       C. How you feel when you think about or are with your lover

10. When meeting someone you want them to:
       A. Look you in the eye
       B. Speak up so you can hear them
       C. Have a solid handshake

Now count up the total number of each answer, A, B, and C and record below:

Total # of A's: _____
Total # of B's _____
Total # of C's _____

Whichever letter you scored the highest in most likely indicates your sensory system preference. We all have five senses, and most often we prefer one over the others to communicate with.

A score high in A's indicates a preference for the visual system.

A score high in B's indicates a preference for the auditory system.

A score high in C's indicates a preference for the kinesthetic system.

> Learn different systems and switch them at will. Some of you can feel that this is unnatural, others will hear the truth of this, and still others will see what we are saying...... Now switch these around: see what you are hearing, feel what you are seeing......

The corollary to having a preferred system is that you may have a weak system, or one that you tend to discount or ignore.

It's a good idea to begin to recognize how you prioritize your representational systems.

For example, if you are most comfortable with visual language and your internal pictures and movies, you may miss important internal communication in the form of your internal dialogue. Or you may get deep into your feelings and not notice what is playing on the inner screen of your mind.

Oftentimes people wish to develop their intuitive abilities, thinking that they don't have any of *that* type of inner communication.

More usually, though, it already exists and isn't being paid attention to. Some people can "see" the future and imagine an outcome. Some may "feel" the best decision, while others may have an inner voice that "tells" them what the right direction is. *Your intuition may not be in the same system that you normally use to communicate with.*

> Understand that your unconscious self—or higher self, or intuition—may be communicating to you in ways you hadn't paid attention to.
>
> *What will it be like in the future to further become aware of, develop and utilize this valuable information **now**?* Is all of this in good taste?

Balancing your systems will increase your flexibility in communicating with others, and may open up new levels of available internal/intuitive information as well.

The easiest way to balance your systems is to practice using your other systems in your language.

If you are primarily visual, simply switch the visual words to auditory and kinesthetic words.

If you are primarily auditory or kinesthetic, practice using the other two systems. There are many "see," "hear" and "feel" words and phrases to choose from. It may seem uncomfortable at first, *and that means you're learning.*

Examples of visual words and phrases: overlook, see through, imagine, view, perspective, focus, bright, colorful, flashy, sparkle, eyesore, disappear, illustrate, reflect, examine, looks familiar, get the picture, see what you're saying. Visual people also tend to talk quickly and use hand gestures.

Examples of auditory words and phrases: comment, listen in, tune out, earful, harmony, noise, call attention to, last word, loud, quiet, yelling, shouting, sounds good, hear what you mean. Auditory people tend to use a lot of words and lengthy explanations, and sometimes make noises and sound effects.

Examples of kinesthetic words and phrases: pressure, pushy, hot, cold, get a feeling for, trust your gut, numb, feel out, handful, to stomach it, jumpy, grasp, get a hold of, put your finger on, weigh options, hammer/drive home, take a stand, stick to it. Kinesthetic people tend to touch and rub things, like their hair, clothes and things with texture.

The field of Neuro-Linguistic Programming (NLP) is primarily responsible for developing this information, and there are many books that go further in depth to develop and utilize it.

Chapter 10

Interlude

It was important to first cover the material we have so far because now we arrive at an important point: We disprove the "reality" of who we *think* we are, we learn how our brain works, and we learn how to be kind to ourselves as we are learning...all **so you can** *take yourself off the hook.*

> **Why is it so important to take yourself off the hook?**

We want to be able to see where we are at this point in time—and *be ok with it*—without generating any value judgment about ourselves. Then we can determine where we would like to be, and create and execute plans to reach those ends.

The ends are infinitely easier to reach if the destination we seek is *not* one that makes us ok, because this is impossible.

We are already ok, *you are already ok,* and if we believe that someone else will add anything to our true being, then we are mistaken.

> Hermann Hesse says in his book *Siddhartha* that Siddhartha had not been able to find his true self, because he had been trying to catch it in the net of thought.

If we think that something outside of us will add something to us, then…no matter where we go or who we become…there is something wrong with us, there is something that can be taken away. On top of that, if we do convince ourselves, we prove that it is possible to be broken.

We are constantly struggling between our factual existence and our infinite ability to use our imagination and fantasize. *The reality of who you are is completely different than the reality of what you can't do. (Some people believe there is no you at all, only many you's… What do you think?)*

> The key: first, be free of self-condemnation; then, act and observe the results you get.

What you say to yourself about who you are is not worth much—except that that your useless self-talk often prevents you from doing what is best for you.

In the end, what counts are the actions and behaviors we engage in; *that* is what gets us our results.

What you do, how you do it and how you make adjustments and improvements along the way to get the results and outcomes you want is "real success"—or at least the path to it. Then, when you finally reach "real success," you may *discover something* **about yourself** *that is far more valuable than any goal you can ever attain.*

It will be infinitely easier to work on goals that come from your own self-acceptance than on goals that "will finally make you OK."

To repeat:

It will be infinitely easier to work on goals that come from your own self-acceptance than on goals that "will finally make you OK."

If you start out with the presupposition that *you are already OK— that you are already complete just as you are—*

then all that you do—all of your goals and projects—will take on a new glow.

There will be a new kind of energy around you, and you will begin to attract the resources and opportunities that enhance you.

If you look closely at your actions, behaviors and emotional reactions, you will get an accurate assessment of "who" you are being. (Stated more accurately, *"who you are doing."*)

This can be very painful at times, which is why it is so important to learn how to look at these parts of yourself without internal subjective judgment (which normally leads to self-hatred and self-punishment).

> Who is this perfect one in you that is doing the hating? What makes her so special?

Our goal up to this point has been to give you the insight and understanding to be able to look at yourself objectively (as much as this is possible) and *say to yourself "OK, I did the best I could at the time. Now...what is it that I really want for myself?"*

You will know that you haven't sufficiently taken yourself off the hook because, when you look at yourself, you will feel discomfort. You may deny it, become angry, frustrated, or feel depressed. This is nothing to be concerned about... It's OK. Just realize that you are in the process of changing, learning and evolving, and *if those feelings come up, remind yourself that you have joined a select elite group of people who are doing something different for themselves instead of merely talking and complaining. You are observing and you are doing.*

> **Separate right now—once and for all—the idea of who you are from the idea of what you do.**

> The caterpillar goes about its business, and lives the life that it knows—the life of the caterpillar. At some point in its life, it begins to build a cocoon around itself... It closes itself off from the outside world for a little while...closes itself off from outside influences and opinions. And while it is inside the darkness, it becomes acquainted with its true self, and out of this true self, without anything being added from the outside, without any education from the external, comes the butterfly.

The caterpillar looks at its own caterpillar reflection, and sees within itself the butterfly inside. It then begins to do what is necessary to become what it already is. This is so in nature, and you are a part of the very same nature...

See your own greatness in your reflection, right now, wherever you find yourself, and begin to do likewise, as the caterpillar does.

Chapter 11

Self-Analysis And What You Want

To help you become a more powerful and effective person and *bring out your best possible strengths*, it is important to assess your present and latent strengths. While the information of this analysis is not written in stone, it will give you a perspective of how to continue to develop your style, updating it where needed.

A chisel is a sculptor's tool, and many sculpt in marble and granite. At first it can seem almost impossible for a beginning sculptor to create something out of such a hard, impervious material. A chisel (or the sculptor, for that matter) does not complete a sculpture in one stroke, or in one pass, but in constant tapping and shaping, as one takes a step back to examine the progress and continues to make adjustments until it is just fine.

It is important to determine what you want for yourself. Most likely you have spent enough time thinking about what you don't like and what you don't want. This will not get you where you want to go.

> If you want to get to New York, it won't help to focus on where you are and what you don't like about not being there yet. Instead of focusing on what you don't want and don't have, it is important to *begin to focus on what you want.*

We will begin to elicit your strengths by analyzing what you are doing now. As you analyze and synthesize the results, you then *begin to increase your flexibility.*

In this section we have provided a disparity coefficient meter as a method for finding out where you are *now.* **You are to do this without judgment.** The items I have included are primary factors. Feel free to add some of your own "areas" into the mix.

Answer these questions truthfully. That is, not what you believe you should have, or your personal ideal—but what you are *now.* This is your baseline......and base it must be......

I am not going to tell you what to do with your results until you are done taking the survey......

The questions underlying each seven point scale are for personal reflection. Come back to them later.

For each factor, circle one of the numbers below:

Intelligence
Low 1 2 3 4 5 6 7 High
How do you know your answer is factual?
How factual do you think it is?

Knowledge
Low 1 2 3 4 5 6 7 High
How do you know your answer is factual?
How factual do you think it is?

Wealth
Low 1 2 3 4 5 6 7 High
How do you know your answer is factual?
How factual do you think it is?

Sex
Low 1 2 3 4 5 6 7 High
How do you know your answer is factual?
How factual do you think it is?

Health
Low 1 2 3 4 5 6 7 High
How do you know your answer is factual?
How factual do you think it is?

Motivation
Low 1 2 3 4 5 6 7 High
How do you know your answer is factual?
How factual do you think it is?

Education
Low 1 2 3 4 5 6 7 High
How do you know your answer is factual?
How factual do you think it is?

Special Skills
Low 1 2 3 4 5 6 7 High
How do you know your answer is factual?
How factual do you think it is?

Attractiveness
Low 1 2 3 4 5 6 7 High
How do you know your answer is factual?
How factual do you think it is?

Social Skills
Low 1 2 3 4 5 6 7 High
How do you know your answer is factual?
How factual do you think it is?

Resistance to Anxiety and Fear
Low 1 2 3 4 5 6 7 High
How do you know your answer is factual?
How factual do you think it is?

Resistance to Depression
Low 1 2 3 4 5 6 7 High
How do you know your answer is factual?
How factual do you think it is?

Personal Power
Low 1 2 3 4 5 6 7 High
How do you know your answer is factual?
How factual do you think it is?

Enlightenment
Low 1 2 3 4 5 6 7 High
How do you know your answer is factual?
How factual do you think it is?

Other
Use as many of these as you need

Now that you are finished, add all of the individual scores and come up with a total score. Divide this number by the number of questions you answered... Be sure to include the "other" category(s) if you used some of your own.

NOW, put this non-book down for a while, take a break, have a snack.

Now take this version of the Disparity Test, but this time, circle the number which represents what you **WANT**......
Circle one of the numbers below

Intelligence
Low 1 2 3 4 5 6 7 High
Is this desire highly probable?
How hard are you willing to work at achieving your
     goal or at least approximating it?
What actions are you going to take?

Knowledge
Low 1 2 3 4 5 6 7 High
Is this desire highly probable?
How hard are you willing to work at achieving your
    goal or at least approximating it?
What actions are you going to take?

Wealth
Low 1 2 3 4 5 6 7 High
Is this desire highly probable?
How hard are you willing to work at achieving your
    goal or at least approximating it?
What actions are you going to take?

Sex
Low 1 2 3 4 5 6 7 High
Is this desire highly probable?
How hard are you willing to work at achieving your
    goal or at least approximating it?
What actions are you going to take?

Health
Low 1 2 3 4 5 6 7 High
Is this desire highly probable?
How hard are you willing to work at achieving your
    goal or at least approximating it?
What actions are you going to take?

Motivation
Low 1 2 3 4 5 6 7 High
Is this desire highly probable?
How hard are you willing to work at achieving your
    goal or at least approximating it?
What actions are you going to take?

Education
Low 1 2 3 4 5 6 7 High
Is this desire highly probable?

How hard are you willing to work at achieving your
   goal or at least approximating it?
What actions are you going to take?

Special Skills
Low 1 2 3 4 5 6 7 High
Is this desire highly probable?
How hard are you willing to work at achieving your
   goal or at least approximating it?
What actions are you going to take?

Attractiveness
Low 1 2 3 4 5 6 7 High
Is this desire highly probable?
How hard are you willing to work at achieving your
   goal or at least approximating it?
What actions are you going to take?

Social Skills
Low 1 2 3 4 5 6 7 High
Is this desire highly probable?
How hard are you willing to work at achieving your
   goal or at least approximating it?
What actions are you going to take?

Resistance to Anxiety and Fear
Low 1 2 3 4 5 6 7 High
Is this desire highly probable?
How hard are you willing to work at achieving your
   goal or at least approximating it?
What actions are you going to take?

Resistance to Depression
Low 1 2 3 4 5 6 7 High
Is this desire highly probable?
How hard are you willing to work at achieving your
   goal or at least approximating it?
What actions are you going to take?

Personal Power
Low 1 2 3 4 5 6 7 High
Is this desire highly probable?
How hard are you willing to work at achieving your
    goal or at least approximating it?
What actions are you going to take?

Enlightenment
Low 1 2 3 4 5 6 7 High
Is this desire highly probable?
How hard are you willing to work at achieving your
    goal or at least approximating it?
What actions are you going to take?

Other
Use as many of these as you need.

Now that you are finished, add up all of the individual
scores and come up with a total score. Divide this number
by the number of questions answered... Be sure to include
the "other" category(s) if you used some of your own......
    Subtract the average score from the first survey from
the average score on the second... This number is your
average Disparity Coefficient. *Do this for each individual
question to see where the greatest disparities occur.*
    Check your results with your own experience. Are the
categories with the greatest gaps the ones that haunt you
the most?
    Are these the areas in which your greatest challenges
lie?
    Are these the areas that—when you make changes in
them—will bring you the most power, relief, joy, and self-
esteem? *Are these the areas that—as you begin working on
them—will allow you to see your true self with greater clarity?*

Back to the Math. Here's an example: where you are
now has an overall score of 3 and what you *want* has an
overall score of 2; your Disparity Coefficient is -1. This

indicates that you are better off than where you'd like to be. "What," you say?

You have either misread the instructions, made a mistake, or you are a masochist or a martyr who has been brainwashed into believing that less is more.

O.K., for real now!

If your average score of what you have now is 3 and your mean score of what you want is 5, your Disparity Coefficient is +2. This is your goal for improvement......

Now determine the Disparity Coefficient for each individual question. Any question which has a difference score of +2 or more requires work. For example, on the intelligence scale, your "have now" score is 3 and what you want is 6; your Disparity Coefficient is +3... Ask yourself: is this realistic and, if so, what might you have to do to approximate the score of 6? (Remember, a 5 is all you really need... How do I know this? From direct observation.)

Take a break and think about this: Do people not automatically measure themselves against some standard all the time? *Are you using your own standards and are they realistic?*

Now go back and use the questions under each scale to see how realistic you are.

Doing this exercise, thinking about what you want, may have stirred up some feelings. You might want to use the techniques from Chapter 8 now.

GETTING WHAT YOU WANT IS OFTEN THE FASTEST PATH TO GROWTH AND HEALING!!!

Chapter 12

Making Changes

Whatever behavior is unacceptable to you **now** can be changed once you deeply understand the many useful purposes it has served in the past. This knowledge does not have to be communicated verbally or even experienced consciously for essential change to take place. For practice, choose any behavior that is **now** unacceptable to you and make a list of up to three useful purposes it once served.

You will want to dedicate a full page (or more) to each thing you want to change. This allows you to keep all corresponding notes, thoughts and progress together.

Please read this chapter through at least once before beginning the exercises in the next chapter. If any thoughts come up that you want to remember, write them down in your notebook or journal.

State a behavior that is **now** unacceptable to you, and write it down in your notebook or journal. This could be a behavior that you have and don't want, or a behavior that you want and have trouble doing.

Then write down three possible useful purposes it once served. For a behavior that you have trouble with, write down the purposes it serves for you not to be able to do it.

Unacceptable or Avoided Behavior:
>>Useful Purpose 1:
>>Useful Purpose 2:
>>Useful Purpose 3:

When you think of the behavior you don't like, most likely there will be a corresponding feeling. Behind this feeling is a belief. You may have to go inside and ask. Write it down.

Feeling:

Remember that sometimes it is difficult to admit to having certain beliefs, patterns and behaviors. Of course, you don't want them to be true of you. If you find yourself getting angry, argumentative or defensive, that is good. It means that you are close. If you are *absolutely positively* **sure** that it's not **that** one, then it probably is. **Just be open and honest with yourself.** If you played it safe and need to adjust the underlying belief, rewrite it and *be honest.*

Belief:

The whole point is to stop hiding these things from yourself, to stop and look at the skeleton chasing you, and decide right now that it's time for something new. Most of the problem with problems is that they are outside of your awareness. *Bringing them into your awareness* may not always be pleasant, but it is *much better* than living your entire life hamstrung by them!

Next, write down what you want. In my opinion, this is the single most important step. The more specific you can be, the better. If it is difficult to be specific, or if you aren't sure, then set a direction to go in.

Next write down a new *preferred* behavior that will move you toward what you want **and** *meet your useful purpose(s).* Write this in terms of a process. Examples: I am now learning to [new behavior] more every day.

Preferred Behavior:

Write down your preferred belief next, as if it is already true about you. Example: I am ok just the way I am, and I'm improving every day.

New Belief:

Begin changing any behavior which is unacceptable to you **now,** but which has served a useful purpose then. Begin by adding something new to your life that has nothing to do with the behavior you want to change. Yes, you read the sentence correctly. The first step in changing any behavior is to add some new behavior to your life that has nothing to do with what you now find unacceptable. Write that down next.

New Unrelated Behavior:

For example when I (Dr. Hyatt) decided that smoking was now unacceptable behavior, I began washing my hands vigorously the first thing in the morning. You might ask yourself how something like this can serve a useful function.

Mind and body parallel each other. This is technically—but somewhat incorrectly—called psycho-physical parallelism. Every event in the body is paralleled by an event in the mind and every event in the mind is paralleled by an event in the body. We know this fact from physiological and biochemical analysis, learning, and hypnotic studies. The so-called placebo effect reflects the workings of this marvelous process. Disregarding the other symbolic aspects of washing my hands, the new act itself *is* at some level *communicating that replacement behavior is now occurring.*

Having dedicated some time to reflect and write, you have put down some important and useful information in your notebook or journal.

This may be the first time you have thought of this and put it all down in one place. Now *things are getting clearer,* allowing you to develop a new perspective of yourself and your possibilities. *You* might even *start feeling more relief, hope and motivation now.*

You can take a look at where you are, you have an understanding of how you got here, you understand the useful purpose your old beliefs and behaviors served, and can accept them because of it. You can accept them and yourself as you are, right now, because you know what you want to accomplish, and you are identifying the new beliefs and behaviors it will take. *It is a significant accomplishment to have just said this about yourself.*

You will be using this information along with the companion CDs and DVDs. Your journal should now look like this:

Unacceptable or Avoided Behavior:

  Useful Purpose 1:

  Useful Purpose 2:

  Useful purpose 3:

Feeling:

Belief:

Preferred Behavior:

New Belief:

New Unrelated Behavior:

After you complete this exercise, having gone inside and done some writing, treat yourself to something. Take a nap, have a treat, be nice to yourself.

Chapter 13

Energized Exercises

You Think You Know Who You Are!

Drawing By MobiusFrame

The following two exercises are designed to open up your unconscious mind, exposing beliefs which you can analyze and gently reformulate.

THE FACE

You are very familiar with your face. You do things to it everyday, but do you know it well enough to know what it is doing behind your back?

At the beginning of this chapter is a picture of the *homunculus*.

It is sitting on a device which is where many of your old beliefs and behaviors belong. (A sense of humor is a good thing…go ahead and *laugh.*)

The features of the homunculus are proportioned to show the relative amount of brain-sensory area dedicated to a particular body part. Study the picture carefully. How aware are you that your face is programming your brain? How aware are you that your face is tracing your past memories?

The face is significantly overrepresented in the brain compared to its actual physical size. Is this a clue to something? Yes! Are you willing to move your face behind your back? Go ahead, give it a try.

Before you begin your self programming and self hypnosis, we are going to show you a few techniques that are designed to open up your bio-neurological channels. You have already learned that much of mind-body communication is non-verbal. The following exercises are specifically designed to open up those channels and to *push the pause button on the old, stuck routines, beliefs and programs.*

Sit down if you like; or if you prefer, stand up and look into the mirror. Just let it go. Move your face any way you like. Or make it stiff if you like. Before you go deeply into yourself, make a face or two, or go wild—or remain stiff, rigid, letting nothing happen.

For six minutes or so you can make every face imaginable or you can hold it stiff, let nothing move, no twitches, do not even blink or simply let it fall. Relax for a moment,

now make as many faces as you can think of that reflect
your various emotions and—?

Do not forget to use the forehead, nose and jaw. Keep
on twisting or holding steady. When you are done you
should feel tingling in your face, more alert and alive.

NOW SENSE AND FEEL

This exercise seems so simple that you may have been
have tempted to try it earlier in your work.

This exercise has immense power even though it
appears almost benign.

The power of this simple exercise is so great that we
have seen people thrown into full blown anxiety after just
a few minutes. At the other extreme, we have seen people
who were so guarded in life that the exercise had no effect
at all, and only served to help the student practice his
nature of not being in touch with his body.

Lie flat on the bed. Breathe normally. There's no
special need to breath deeply, but you might want to take
a few deep breaths and sigh a few times. Now, make **NO**
voluntary movements. **NONE.**

For one full hour talk out loud, reporting on sensations
from your body. It is critical for this exercise that you not
let even a moment pass without saying something. If you
have to, simply repeat the report you just made or use
some vocal pause sound (uh, uh, uh…) to make sure that
you never stop talking. We don't want you to fall asleep
NOW.

Don't bother to set an alarm clock to measure the hour;
do it for what you think must be an hour; then stop and
check the clock afterwards. Don't check the clock and
restart the exercise to get in an hour. However long you do
the exercise, that is the time that will be spent.

A session might start with a full scan of your body.
Here is a made-up example:

"My forehead is flat, my eyes seem stuck in the middle
of my head, I can't feel any tension in my jaw but there is a

lot of saliva, my neck feels normal, there is a pressure on my chest as if there were a weight on it, I can feel the bed beneath my fingers and there seems to be a slight kind of tingle in my right wrist, my diaphragm feels a little like it is quivering, my abdomen feels empty like there's a balloon inside it taking up the space, I am aware of my genitals, my thighs feel tight, there is a tingling in both knees, my right calf is tighter than my left calf, I can't feel anything in my feet."

After you've gone over the whole body once, you can do it again to see if there are any changes; or you can focus on one thing (for example, the tingling in the knees) and see if and how the sensation changes. If you are focusing on one part of the body and it is not changing at all then leave that part and turn to some other part, or to a full body report.

It does not matter if you have nothing to report. It only matters that you do not let yourself stop talking and that you continue to focus on the sensations from your body.

GOING DEEPER NOW

This is a more advanced version of the "Sense and Feel" exercise. As such it should not be done until you have rung everything you can from the basic exercise.

Now that you have done the basic exercise a number of times and are good at sensing your body, we are ready for this next step. Here, after sensing your body as usual, you pick an area of tension or other sensation, and you start to manipulate the sensation.

If it is tingling, you may try to spread the tingling to more of the body. If it is tension, you may try to increase the tension, or you may try to relax that part of the body.

If you have a part of the body that has no sensation, is dead, try to put sensation into that part of the body.

When you have modified an area of sensation, just watch it and report. Never stop talking. Don't forget issues like pleasant or unpleasant, scary or calming, hot or cold, alive or dead, light or heavy, etc. Just report everything you can sense, stay with the body, and never let yourself stop talking out loud.

€V€N D€€P€R?

We come now to another exercise. To get the most out of this one, you should have a tape recorder. With a recorder, you can be concerned only with your own body and emotions—and, as you will see, memories—and not be concerned with what you say. The recorder will capture what you say and you will listen to the tape after the session is over.

By the time you get here you will have already done at least half a dozen simple "sense, feel, report" sessions. You have also freed up at least your forehead and eyes using the face exercise above.

Having reached this level of your nature, you may have already noticed that you are far more emotional and, at the same time, far more able to control your emotions. Let's amplify the last one.

We have emphasized that feelings and thoughts will arise during sessions and that they are to be *allowed to have their expression* without your trying to suppress them.

At this late stage, we are going to mention another change that is likely to have happened.

You've probably heard all your life that emotions are irrational. Surprise, they re not! Emotions are as rational as all of the rest of our being. But, more important than their rationality, is that they are subject to our will: that is, **they are subject to our conscious, willed control**. We are not going to go deeply into how and why this is so, although the following example may help illustrate this.

If you have had children, you have probably done this yourself; you just did not think about the general implications of doing it. Consider a young child. The child is depressed or hurt and is crying. You say to the child, "Now let me see a smile." You finally get the child to put on a voluntary smile and the crying stops. You say to the child, "Now that's better, you feel better now don't you."

The child either agrees or kind of nods **yes**. What is the general implication of that little scene?

Well, crying and smiling are opposites. Humans can't use the smile muscles of the face, and at the same time cry. One feeling fights and stops the other feeling.

But there is a much broader principle involved: we can, in fact, control our feelings by willful choices. Sometimes that willful choice involves imposing other emotions and/ or body actions; but that is only the technique, it is not the principle as such. The principle is that, in the last analysis, our feelings are under our volitional control. One of the changes in yourself that you should have noticed by now is that your feelings, when they occur, are (1) stronger, (2) more pure, and (3) more able to be controlled.

If you have not noticed that last point, that feelings are now more subject to your will, then take a few weeks and pay attention to that fact. We don't mean that your feelings are now arbitrary or that you don't sometimes have a mood that you can not seem to shake off; what we do mean is that when something happens to which you normally react with a given feeling or set of feelings, that now you are much more able to set aside that feeling when it is not appropriate.

There is a simple way to illustrate this. You have just been stopped by a policeman who is going to issue you a traffic citation. Now, there are two very common ways that people react to this situation: one is anger and the other is self-pity. Obviously anger is inappropriate, at least while the policeman is by your car. That policeman has a gun, a night stick and mace. No matter what anger you might be feeling, it is not very clever to express it to the policeman. Likewise, with self-pity. The policeman is not going to be influenced by your sad story. If your long-winded explanation annoys him, you may be inviting him to give you a second citation.

So, wisdom dictates that you willfully keep your feelings in check until the policeman is gone. If the expression of feelings were not under willful control you could not do that.

One of the great benefits of being able to control or set aside a feeling is that *you now no longer have to fear them.*

Long ago in this non-book we mentioned that most people are terrified by their own anger. (Did we mention that? Or have you forgotten? Or did we forget?) They don't get angry as much as they become afraid—of their own anger reaction. But now, if you have come far enough, gone deep enough, you have seen that you can control your anger or any other emotion. You can let the feelings out or you can suppress them. You no longer have to fear feelings because you have experienced that they are under your willful control—you can let them have free reign and then stop them completely whenever you wish.

Now, for this most advanced exercise, we are going to introduce another fact: that feelings are seldom singular. It is seldom the case that our body manifests only a single emotion. Feelings differ in intensity, and most people are mostly incapable of recognizing (that is, naming) any more than the most intense feelings. But, as you free body area after body area, you become more and more able to sense and name ever more of the subtle feelings. We usually use half a dozen feelings as a rough goal. That is, at any one moment we search for half a dozen ongoing feelings (body states).

Above we spoke about fear as a reaction to anger. That is, many people fear their own anger. That means that the fear and anger are both present at the same time.

But, after all, the anger is there for a reason. Maybe it is annoyance or frustration. That is a third feeling. You are annoyed or frustrated about something. You are annoyed because someone interrupted what you were doing or you are frustrated because you were prevented from doing something you wanted to do. So, that annoyance or frustration is mingled with feeling sorry for yourself. You have a fourth feeling.

But being interrupted or prevented from doing something means that the person who imposed on you does not understand you. You are feeling misunderstood and almost invisible, as though you do not matter. Now we have feelings five and six.

You get the idea. The more you become sensitive to yourself, the more you are able to identify your mix of feelings. That ability will, in turn, affect your dreams which will change your nature.

Now we are going to make use of all these facts and abilities in this exercise.

EVEN DEEPER AND DEEPER NOW

This exercise is designed to identify feelings. Use the tape recorder to monitor everything you say so that you do not have to be distracted from your main task.

You have already learned to sense your body including all the subtle experiences like tension or lightness or various other sensations. The next step is to put an emotive-like name to each body experience.

We say "emotive-like" because it is not necessarily an emotion. It might be an action-like phrase or a state-like phrase. Here are some examples. You feel tension in your calves. Now you try to put a name to that tension. It could be that the calf wants to run, or it wants to play a game like jump-rope, or it wants to bend and pull tight against your thigh. For each and every one of those actions your calf seems to want to do, you give it an emotive-like name or description.

Of course, all of the above are only examples. You will find your own areas of tension or lack of feeling around the body and come up with the best descriptions and/or names you can.

As always, don't rush. Do not attempt to be a super pupil. *Take your time and do them thoroughly.* The better you become at spotting and naming areas of activity—or the absence of activity—in a body area, the more you can more use of the next step.

OK, you have gotten fairly good at naming. Now add the next step. You identify the area of sensation, you name it, then you manipulate it. Recall that this variation of the "sense, feel, report" exercise involves being able to manipulate your body sensations.

So now we add this ability to our arsenal of personal power. The major goal is still the same: naming. But now you are going to name the initial sensation and then modify it. You can modify it by increasing it, decreasing it, or moving it to another area of the body. Once you have changed the intensity or the location you are going to name it all over again.

Here is a made-up example. You notice that your chest feels constricted, tight. You take that tightness and move it to your abdomen. Now it feels like disgust. You take that disgust and move it to your face. Now it feels like disdain. Now you go back to your chest to find that the tightness has become longing.

Don't forget the point we made above. At any given moment there are about a half dozen ongoing feelings or desires in your body. Acknowledge one, name, manipulate and rename; then go on to a second one. If you can't spot a second one immediately, simply rescan the whole body; but, as always don't allow yourself to stop talking aloud even for a moment.

YES, THERE IS EVEN MORE

Here we draw on all the abilities you have developed so far and, using those abilities, we move to another step. Here you are going to employ—or rather, allow—associations which you will report out load and let the tape recorder save for you.

What do we mean here by "associations"? We mean that any thought that happens to enter your mind while you are doing this exercise is followed and reported out loud. Caution: these thoughts are not, on the whole, practical issues (like how can I handle that task at work or what am I going to do about the kids); rather, they are random thoughts that originate from sensing and/or manipulating your body and which seem to have no immediate relevance to your life.

Here's an example. Of course, you would have said all of this out loud to be recorded so that you can play back and analyze the material later.

"My right hand wants to ball up into a fist. What does it want to do? I don't know. What does it want to do? It doesn't so much want to make a fist as it just wants to close the fingers against the top of the hand so that my hand is not open. Maybe I don't want to shake hands. Let's see what comes to mind. Yes, I recall when my father introduced me to some famous man and I just said 'hi' and my father later balled me out for not being more respectful. But I didn't know. It was just another adult. How often have I been criticized for not acting some way when I did not even know I was supposed to act that way? Yes, it used to happen all the time. I was always wrong for doing things that I thought were proper, and then I would get criticized for not doing it someone else's way. I just thought of my third grade teacher. She used to do that to me all the time and I felt so inadequate and so embarrassed that I tried not to do anything. Is that why my grades in school were not good? Maybe I started using that 'hold back' pattern in all of school? I don't know. It may be. But then I think of Justin. Justin always liked me. He didn't tell me that I was doing things wrong. You know, it occurs to me in one way or another that all my life I have been trying to find other Justins. I have always sought approval and praise only because I assumed I was doing things wrong like daddy and the teacher said and I have always expected the criticism unless I got praise. Now I understand why I didn't take that job, I thought I was too likely to make mistakes there and again it would be just like daddy yelling at me for an error I didn't even know I was making............"

That is free association. You allow your mind to go from one idea to another with no control or censorship. Whatever comes into your mind gets reported and it is all recorded.

Then, after the session, you listen to the tape and you can reflect on what you have learned about yourself and your nature.

FINALLY, DEEP SLEEP?

Some people will be very good at this exercise while others will struggle. There is no good or bad implication to either the ease or the struggle. It is simply the way your brain operates and is not something over which you have control or can change. Simply accept that this is easy or hard for you and let it go at that.

This technique starts with the ability to sense and name areas of sensation in the body. Here are the steps.

1. Find an area of sensation (usually tension).

2. Name the held emotions or action tendency. Generally there are two good ways to do this. One is to ask yourself what that part of the body would want to do if it had its own will. The other is to visualize a blackboard where a word or phrase gets magically written.

3. Grow that particular sensation such that it spreads over the whole body. Don't fight this, just do the best you can. Perhaps think of it like a can of paint that has been dumped over that area of tension and the paint is gradually spreading over your whole body. If your arms want to hit, then your whole body feels like it wants to hit. If your arms want to come across your chest in a hiding, protective posture, then your whole body wants to contract, shrink, hide and be invisible.

4. Once you have spread the sensation or feeling over your whole body, then hold that state, and re-sense your whole body to find a new area of sensation.

5. Spread that new tension over your whole body.

6. At this point, in most cases, a long-forgotten memory will come to you. If you don't get a memory at this point, then repeat steps 4 and 5. If you still don't get a memory, then forget the exercise for this session—it is not being productive.

The memory tells you a lot about yourself. First, it is the time when these two (or more) feelings occurred together. An example: embarrassed and stupid; angry and futile; unhappy and stubborn; etc.

Next, as you examine these two (or more) feelings in your life, you may be able to see how that recovered scene (recovered memory) has in one form or another been repeated innumerable times in your life.

It may be something minor, explaining, for example, why you are unwilling to try new foods. It may be something that explains a pattern of your life, such as why you keep getting fired from jobs. Or it may be something major like why you choose to get a bureaucratic job instead of getting a job in the productive sector. If you have children, it may explain why you act the way you do toward them.

In any event that recovered memory will give you a window, big or small, into your nature and why you have lived the life you have.

After completing these exercises you may have more insight and wish to add to your work from Chapter 12.

Chapter 14

The CDs & DVDs

Now it is time to work with the companion audio CDs and video DVDs. *You* have your beliefs and behaviors picked out, you know what you want to develop. Think about what it feels like to have already succeeded in making those changes. Think about what your life *will* be like in the future, with all of those new beliefs, skills, abilities and good feelings, *NOW*.

Remember to go through your exercises before listening so you *receive the maximum benefits and personal change.*

Work with the companion material in a comfortable place, sitting comfortably or lying down. Make sure you won't be interrupted. Turn off your telephones and anything else that makes noise. You have worked hard up to this point, so make the most of your experience.

Chapter 15

Parting Thoughts

You have read the non-book, listened to the CDs and watched the DVDs. You are making changes. Using the power of your mind you have begun to re-learn and re-groove old beliefs, behaviors and patterns into more effective ones.

Continue to watch and practice.

You will have to make decisions.

Watch your emotions as they come up and go, and remember to differentiate between those that come from your old brain and old patterns (feel and decide without thinking), and those that come from your new ability to *think and decide while feeling*. Keep in mind that feelings only feel like they are true because that is their purpose.

Your feelings are communication from another part of you. Step back and watch, *then* decide if they are true about the here-and-now, or whether they are coming from the past. If they are coming from the past, and you use them, you will get more of your past. If this is not what you want, then *focus on what you want NOW*. Most of what you are doing is simply rising above your old programming and the associated feelings from it, and reprogramming in a way that gets you what you want now.

> The little girl mentioned in Chapter 3 did just that, and now she tries all kinds of new things, continues to learn and grow, started her own business and drinks orange juice whenever she likes.

Remember to *separate who you are from what you do.*

You will make mistakes from time to time. Learn from them. They give you valuable knowledge and experience. You are not your actions, your past experiences or your story, so keep yourself off the hook.

Keep on the lookout for that hook, and any time you are about to label yourself and make a generalization about your value or worth, say "No. I am fine the way I am, and I no longer need any negative concepts, feelings, beliefs or behaviors to guide me any more." *You decide. You choose. Be respectful to yourself.* Remember that any negative or positive metaphysical statements about you are nonsense. You don't need them anymore.

Every day, start where you are, right now. *Decide to let this be enough.*

Keep the passion and update the information.

Continue to let go of the old beliefs that were programmed into you while you were too uninformed to realize what was going on. You have already given yourself permission, so keep on going.

> The two young men mentioned earlier have also used the information in this book and have gone on to live life fully. Through their own experience they are confident that it can be done, and that **You** can do it, if you choose to. How can they be so sure? They are the authors of this non-book.

Right now is your time, your turn.

The single most important factor for you right now, is to *decide to keep going.*

Keep re-evaluating, re-learning and re-deciding as you go. You will notice that pretty soon you will be doing things that will surprise yourself. You will find that over time, what you are able to accomplish through your changes will seem miraculous to others.

This reminds me of a story about martial arts. What is the difference between the Master and his students? Students practice diligently to attain mastery. To students, the Master appears to be perfect, even superhuman. The students believe in perfection and mastery.

The difference is that the Master realizes that there is no mastery, only practice. Therefore he devotes himself completely to his practice and to the moment. Because he is in the moment, and not measuring himself against perfection, he squeezes incredible amounts of learning and achievement out of his practicing.

He knows that there is no perfection, no destination to arrive at, that there is only the journey. Since he knows there is no destination, he is free from the burden of *"not being there."* And in this knowing, he no longer has the fear of "not good enough." The master believes in the ability to learn, adapt and improvise, knowing that this is always enough, and compared to the average person, more than enough.

The master believes in himself. Why? Because *he/she is*—and, therefore, there is no need to believe.

Appendix A: Inductions

The two inductions which follow are from the DVD *Energized Hypnosis Volume III: Sex & Beyond* (available from http://www.originalfalcon.com).

The General Induction

As you begin to know *now* that you are there,
wherever you choose
you might notice many things
which are familiar——or not
your eyes closing
your shoulders touching
your fingers
your toes
remembering
very pleasant
times—

deeper NOW
like
the last time you felt deeply

at peace—
at wonder
whole

the time you were
in the right place

you were there...

those very precious times
which *NOW* you remember better
as you become more aware—deeply

each inhale
each
exhale
each inhale
deeply aware
each exhale
deeper—awareness

NOW deeper now
maybe a sigh—

deeper memories

being free...
like that new toy
a new friend—
a deep pleasure—
free

those precious first times
so many—now...
whenever you wish

how natural for you
like sleeping deeply—

being good at it
like your first step—
forward
better each time
deeper each time
that wonderful smile

it can be easier each time you try ....
like *NOW*
all those moments
the deeper you go

knowing that there are

so many
times

when
you were free

just to be

deep peace
joyful peace
satisfied
a coming smile

whatever displeased you
simply
vanished
gone—
deeper NOW

you can decide
when and where
here and now

to remember those times
whenever you need them
just at the right moment
remembering when you decide

you can go however deep
you wish
however far

you can do whatever you need to do there
you are able to find everything you need

in that special place

and you may not even notice how much you have
    there
YOU decide
how far you can go

when NOW is always your choice
finding yourself at rest

knowing the resources
are THERE

within *YOU NOW...*

Sexual Union Trancing

while you are here
you can think about love
about the joys you have had
and while you are there
you can imagine what might happen
even more, even closer, even deeper

there is no need to hurry NOW
whatever time you take
is yours

you owe yourself all that time
you can go as deep as you like
slowly,
desire
each time, deeper and deeper
and the accepting of it all
as never before

Melt slowly,
merge deeply
with each breath

sweet feelings
moving through you

as you like it
with each breath
deeper and deeper
slower and slower
hotter and hotter
deeper and deeper
as you let go

there is plenty of time
as much as you like

like that time
when you didn't want it to stop

to never end

and you knew how to make it better
to make it last—deeper
now

you can have wonders
depending on your taste

you will know more later

there is no hurry
only doing what you have learned be-fore
what you have practiced be—fore
freely
differently

each new time, more and better
as you go deeper and feel more inside

there is no worry
only your ecstasy

each moment can be an eternity
let all the eternities—have you.

there are many for you NOW—
Later

Melt slowly,
merge deeply
with each breath

sweet feelings
moving through you

the head tenses and relaxes
the neck and throat follows
the chest deep and full
letting go now
exhaled deep

the belly like jelly
and that deep feeling
below
down low
as you go deeper now

shiver
shake
twitch
letting go
submitting to moments of joy

giving everything
pulse after pulse
wave after wave

finally yours
you are one
with your love
deep love
deep kiss
all given

sleep
now
and dream

as long as you like

awake
Refreshed

Appendix B: Surprises

The Many in the One

You might have noticed throughout the day many yous. It is a good thing to know who is driving the car at any one moment. Most people change drivers throughout the day, and it is good to remember who likes to go fast and who is overcautious. This model will help you identify in others who is in charge at the moment, and it will give you clues on when and how to approach them.

Here are some labels of "who is who." Now remember: these are *metaphors* and don't exist in your brain. (If they did, it would make life way too easy. You could simply get rid of the ones you don't like...)

Nurturing Parent: helpful, protective, supportive, instructive.

Pig Parent: nasty, harsh, judgmental, pushy, demanding, (full of shoulds, have-tos, ought-tos and worse); irrational belief systems.

Adult: rational, matter-of-fact, useful, helpful, social and competent in the real world.

Crazy Child: full of irrational beliefs, acts out, pushy, mean at times, hurtful. (Keep in mind that the crazy child is a result of the Pig Parent.)

Natural child: Playful, inquisitive, friendly, exploratory, laid back at times, adventuresome.

NOW **The Enlightened Observer:** You define this one for yourself: This mode is rare in most people, though if you look around you will find seeds of it in yourself.

THE *Original* FALCON PRESS
Invites You to Visit Our Website:
http://originalfalcon.com

At our website you can:

- Browse the online catalog of all of our great titles
- Find out what's available and what's out of stock
- Get special discounts
- Order our titles through our secure online server
- Find products not available anywhere else including:
  – One of a kind and limited availability products
  – Special packages
  – Special pricing
- Get free gifts
- Join our email list for advance notice of New Releases and Special Offers
- Find out about book signings and author events
- Send email to our authors
- Read excerpts of many of our titles
- Find links to our authors' websites
- Discover links to other weird and wonderful sites
- And much, much more

Get online today at http://originalfalcon.com